Contents

Introduction

Welcome to Living Life to the Full.

I'm Professor Chris Williams, Emeritus Professor of Psychosocial Psychiatry at the University of Glasgow. I've been working for the last 20 years looking at ways of helping people improve their lives.

We can all sometimes feel down or fed up, stressed or worried, or that we aren't good enough. However, there are things you can do to make positive changes in each of these areas. It also involves rediscovering the things you already do that are good for you- and how to build these in your life.

I'm an expert in a talking treatment called cognitive behavioural therapy- or CBT. It is often offered to help people with low mood or stress. It can help prevent problems such as these developing in the first place. Because of this it is increasingly being offered as a way of helping people learn key skills that can give them a growing sense of control over how they feel and react. These are skills that can last a lifetime.

Skills such as these can make a real difference to any of our lives. There are no quick fixes, and to really get good at using the skills will take practice. At times all of us need to learn how to be calmer, more confident and in control, happier and someone others turn to for answers.

Get added support online

We recommend you also register to use the LLTTF course online at **www.llttf.com.** It's a useful added support as you read through this book. It contains a great range of optional modules and resources, as well as the weekly emails you can sign up to that remind and encourage you to read and apply what you're learning.

Other course resources for young people:

www.llttf4children.com
for primary school aged children.

www.llttfyp.com
My Big Life course for years 1/2 (secondary school).

My Big Life (MBL and LLTTF-YP

We have two courses aimed at secondary school-aged young people. My Big Life covers transition (starting secondary school and the first 2 years at High School.

Living Life to the Full for Young People (LLTTF-YP) is designed for older young people at secondary schools. It extends the range of life skills taught, and does so in age appropriate ways.

As you read the book, you can print off any linked worksheets from www.llttf.com/resources to allow you to practice the skills you are learning (free registration). Look out for this BUTTON to highlight these free resources.

Download
from

www.llttf.com/resources

Introduction to Chapter 1

Do you want to change your life?
Most of us from time to time want to make life changes.
Feel happier? Plan to get a holiday job? Improve a
friendship? Bounce back from a disappointment? Be more
confident? Feel less stressed?

How we see and describe change matters.
For example, do we see change as a positive, or difficult and
something to be avoided? Or does it seem too big or hard a
step to even get started?

We need to identify what needs to change and decide where
to start.

This first chapter will help you get into the right frame of
mind to plan and achieve change. It will help build your
motivation and keep you on track.

Sometimes our life journey can seem positive and exciting.
At other times more difficult and challenging. Good or bad,
change happens to us all.

By the end of this chapter you will feel better equipped to
make changes.

Getting added support: Many people use this book on it's
own. It can also be used alongside the **www.llttf.com** web
course which includes weekly support emails.

If you need more help: Reach out and tell someone- a
parent, teacher, friend, brother or sister. Get the help you
need. Don't suffer in silence.

Chapter 1

WANT TO LIVE LIFE TO THE FULL? HERE'S HOW TO GET STARTED

I want things to change

Can this help me?

This is going to be easy

If changing things was easy I'd have done it before!

I'VE NO TIME TO DO IT

I WANT SOMEONE TO TELL ME THE ANSWERS

My problems are too hard to change

I can't afford not to

I don't want to write things down

MAYBE IT'S WORTH A TRY

Helping you help yourself

Congratulations - you're about to change your life!

Not overnight. Not without a lot of work. But you **can** change and you **will** change, if you try out the suggestions here and in the other chapters of this book.

Note we said 'try'. That's the point about this approach when you're down or want to change – you need to work at changing things. This way, you learn a lot about what makes you tick, and the changes you make tend to stick.

But just reading isn't enough.

You've got to go over the content again and again to work it into your life.

Don't worry! You only have to do 15 things and one of them is grabbing a juice or putting the kettle on.

Are you ready for number 1?

THE TIME, THE PLACE, THE CHAIR, THE TEAPOT

Make a space for yourself to learn

You're wanting to change your life. What you're doing is very important and you must treat it that way.

Choose a time and place each day to read your little book. It's your space, your time for changing.

Make it a quiet, comfy place, but not too luxurious. Sitting at a table is better than lounging on the settee, for instance. You're working on your life – don't slouch.

Pour a juice or put the kettle on and make a cup of tea to sip while you're working. And make sure you have two pens and a notebook or paper.

Two pens? So you don't have to stop if one runs out.

Number

Number

2

NO DISTRACTIONS, NO BISCUITS, NO IFS, NO BUTS

You need a clear focus when you're changing your life

Switch off notifications or mute your mobile.

Nibbling is also a distraction. If it's lunchtime, have lunch. Then go to your reading place and work on change.

TV is something else you don't need in the background, as is music. In fact, try to get rid of as much noise as possible.

Shut the windows if you're distracted by traffic noise. Close the door if people are passing by. Switch off the TV, the radio and the PC.

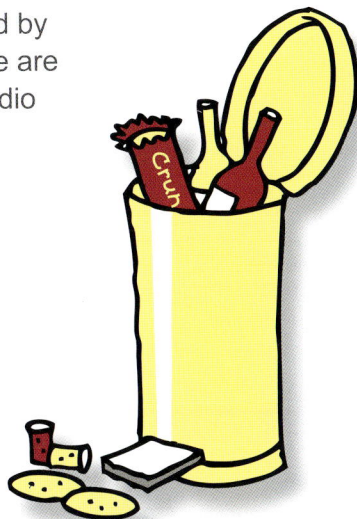

THE
ENERGY
THING

Steal a trick from the movies

Just before they go in front of the camera, a lot of actors run on the spot for a few moments, or press hard against the wall, or trot up and down the stairs.

It gets them energised and adds an extra energy to their performance.

If you do the same before you sit down to work on change, you'll feel livelier and more able to do what it suggests. You'll feel a bit more energetic and positive.

It doesn't really matter what you do, so long as it's something that uses your muscles.

You could do a few press-ups, touch your toes, jump up and down for a minute or so.

If your mobility isn't great, try pushing your hands together or stretching. Use these physical changes to energise your thinking so you're ready for action.

REPEAT IT 'TILL YOU KNOW IT BY HEART

If the book is falling apart, it probably means you aren't *

Don't just read the course resources - really work them into your life.

Read the content carefully and think about what it's saying. Ask yourself "How does this apply to me?" Make a note of words or ideas that help you better understand how you feel. Capture phrases or words that challenge or encourage you.

Learn in the way that suits you best. You might work through things in one longer session. Or do it in a series of shorter reading sessions. It doesn't matter which way you do it, just do it - again and again.

None of our resources have many words for a good reason - so that you can read them over and over until you know them off by heart.

It's very human for us to sometimes forget. So spend time reflecting on what you're learning and write it down in a learning diary - perhaps as a calendar entry or note on your phone. Set reminders there to prompt you to keep applying what you learn.

To do that you need something else ...

*Okay, if you're reading the book online or as an ebook, the pages won't fall out (not unless you drop your phone anyway.) But we hope you get the point.

DON'T JUST SIT THERE, MAKE A PLAN!

How to get what you're learning off the page and into your life

Download from
www.llttf.com/resources

When you've read and read the content and really know it, it's time to make a plan. Decide what you're going to do or change and work out how you'll do it.

Write your plan down, step by step. Be sure to make them small, simple steps that you will be able to do.

Use the Planner sheet on the next two pages. You can download more for free from www.llttf.com/resources

All of the resources in this series include linked worksheets. They have spaces for you to gather information, or put what you are learning into practice. Writing things down is important- it helps us work out what we think, and aids our learning.

Remember, however you are using this- as a printed book, an e-book or online module at www.llttf.com, you're working on changing your life and your regular sessions are about making plans and checking progress.

It's all about learning.

Planner Sheet

Make a Plan!

1. What am I going to do?

Just one small thing

2. When am I going to do it?

That way you'll know if you don't do it

3. What problems or difficulties could happen, and how can I overcome them?

From the:
Living life to the full
resources.

Download from

www.llttf.com/resources

4. Is my planned task -

	Yes	No
• Useful for understanding or changing how I am?	☐	☐
• Specific, so that I will know when I have done it?	☐	☐
• Realistic, practical and achievable?	☐	☐

My notes:

Copyright Five Areas Resources Ltd (2021). Used under licence.
Download more for free from www.llttf.com/resources

THINK ABOUT A CLIMBING WALL

You can do anything if you break it into bits

How do you get to the top of a climbing wall? In lots of small steps.

It's the same with changes to your life. Even if your task looks enormous, you **will** be able to do it if you break it into bits.

Let's say you want to cut down social media use. You could break the week into bits and just stop on Mondays, for example.

If you want to get out more, just work on part of the problem - like leaving the house or walking round the park.

Or if you're spending too much, you could start by just cutting out online shopping.

Most tasks can be broken down like this, and you're much more likely to succeed when you do things bit by bit.

WHAT IF YOU

GET

STUCK?

Don't worry, everyone does

Everybody can get stuck or discouraged from time to time. Nobody can sail straight through an important change in life without feeling fed up or finding it difficult sometimes.

There are two things you must do about this:

1. Expect to get stuck from time to time.

2. Work out what to do about it in advance.

There are lots of things that can help you through the difficult patches.

Check the next point for ideas.

Number

8

ACCEPT THAT CHANGE IS LIKE A NEW YEAR RESOLUTION

And you know what happens to them

We're all the same at New Year. Lots of good intentions, lots of plans to change our lives.

But then, often just a couple of weeks into January, we slip and go back to the same old routines.

Here's what you do to stop your plan turning into a failed resolution:

- Get a diary or your phone and mark the start of your plan.
- Now, mark a Review Day on the same day every week for three months ahead. Why so long? Because you're working at setting up a new routine that sticks for the long-term.
- Once a week, on every Review Day, think about how you're doing. Use the Review Sheet on the next two pages to plan your review.

Use the pattern of *Plan, Do and Review* to help you move forwards.

If you reckon you need more help, get in touch with your school or college guidance teacher, or support worker (if you have one). Or ask trusted friends or relatives to help you stay on track. Signing up for the weekly emails at www.llttf.com might also help.

Over the page is an idea that will help with this.

LTTF™
living
life to
the full
www.llttf.com

Review Sheet

How did it go? What did you plan to do?

Did you try to do it?   Yes ☐   No ☐

If yes: What went well?

What didn't go so well?

What have you learned from what happened?

How are you going to apply what you have learned?

From the:
Living life to the full
resources.

Download from
www.llttf.com/resources

If no: What stopped you?

External things (other people, work or home issues etc.)

Internal things (forgot, not enough time, put it off, didn't think I could do it, couldn't see the point etc.)

How can you tackle things differently next time?

Copyright Five Areas Resources Ltd (2021). Used under licence.
Download more for free from www.llttf.com/resources

Number 9

GET YOUR FRIENDS, FAMILY OR CARERS ON THE TEAM

Don't try and do this alone

The more people you involve in your plan for change, the more likely it is to work out.

Right from the start, tell all the people you trust what you're doing and ask for their support. They'll be there for you when you struggle, or when doubts set in. Phone them up and tell them how you feel.

If you have someone very close – a boyfriend, girlfriend, brother, sister or best friend - you could even do your reading and planning sessions together. When you find things difficult, he or she will remind you why you're doing this and may even tell you things you don't want to hear.

That's what real friends are for.

SIT DOWN AND WRITE YOURSELF A LETTER

Do it now, while you're all fired up

Imagine it's five years from now and you're sitting down to write a thank you letter to yourself.

Life has changed and moved on. You want to thank the person you were five years ago, for persevering, making the changes, sticking with things and keeping working on the future.

What would you write? Get your pen, turn the page and work it out.

Dear

I want to say thanks for sticking with
it five years ago

Keep working on change
- stick in there.
Kind wishes for a better future,
    from Me

(Keep this letter and read it again and again.
It's your future. Don't throw it away).

MAKE

A

NOTE

Remind yourself why you're doing all this

Pepper your fridge with post-it notes.

Write messages on them about why you want to change, what it will be like when you solve your problem, how great you're going to feel when it's done.

Now write some more and stick them in the bathroom, so you see them every morning.

Stick notes on the kitchen cupboards, on the TV and on your desk, locker or PC. Arrange things so that your routine gets you face to face with at least ten messages each day. Plan encouraging reminders into your phone calendar as well so you receive reminders at times you know might be difficult.

And then, once a week, move them around so you don't get so used to seeing them you take no notice.

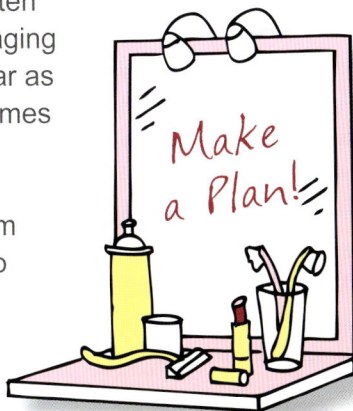

GIVE YOURSELF SOME GOOD ADVICE

What would you say to your best friend?

If you're feeling really stuck, this often works.

Imagine it's not you with the problem, but your best friend. He or she was doing really well but has struggled lately.

What would you say? What warm words of encouragement would you use to remind your friend that things will be better when the problem is sorted? How would you gently encourage him or her to get back on track?

Now say all that to yourself. Give yourself the advice and support that you'd give to your very best friend. You deserve it.

THINK

LIKE

AN

ATHLETE

Download from
www.llttf.com/resources

Get support wherever you can find it

Top athletes know they can't win alone. They look for a great coach and good advice and get help in every way they can.

You're just the same, so look around and get support from as many places as possible. It will help you stay on track and moving forward.

Accept help in any form that's useful - whether it's face to face from a pastoral care or guidance teacher, or other support worker, by telephone, by email, via a reading group, treatment group, friends or family, or from a voluntary sector worker or counsellor.

Like an athlete, you're aiming for a personal best. The more help you get, the more chance you have of making it.

Got a supporter? Use the Agenda on the next page, and the Getting the most from the Session sheet (the page after). You can download it from www.llttf.com/resources.

living
life to
the full
www.llttf.com

Agenda

Download from
www.llttf.com/resources

For discussion dated:

What's going well?

What's not going so well?

What have I learned from this?

How am I putting what I've learned into practice?

After the session, review what you learned

Getting the most out of the session

From the:
Living life to the full resources.

Download from

www.llttf.com/resources

Three key things I have learned:

1.

2.

3.

My Notes:

How can you remember what you have learned?
(Eyes? Ears? Actions?)

My Worksheets:

Putting what you have learned into practice.

My Plan*:

1. What am I going to do?

2. When am I going to do it?

3. What problems or difficulties could
happen, and how can I overcome them?

*Or use the Planner sheet.

Copyright Five Areas Resources Ltd (2021). Used under licence.
Download more for free from www.llttf.com/resources

MORE THINGS THAT WILL HELP YOU

HELP YOURSELF

*Bennion et al, 2017. BMJ Open http://bmjopen.bmj.com/content/7/1/e014844

You can get added help and support by working through the free linked online modules at www.llttf.com. It's an award-winning course, and the number one site for low mood and anxiety recommended by NHS Trusts and teams in England.*

It's also recommended by the NHS Scotland National Wellbeing hub www.promis.scot/resources/coping-and-self-care.

How to get the most from the course

The next four chapters cover core topics such as understanding how you feel, and how to make changes so you feel better.

The remaining chapters of the book cover additional areas such as anger and irritability, the things you do that help, and the things you do that don't, building inner confidence, and things you can do to feel happier straight away. Together the content of the book and course covers all the most common issues that people need to improve their wellbeing.

Introduction to Chapter 2

All of us from time to time feel happy - glad, even joyful. When we feel like this it's a great feeling isn't it?

But sometimes we feel bad. Down, low, sad, stressed, anxious, worried, panicky, angry or embarrassed.

Did you know we feel like we do for a reason? That's what this chapter is about. It provides you with the keys to understanding how you feel.

Have you ever had a bad cold? You notice the runny nose and sore throat, the itchy eyes and the aches, pains and coughs. How we feel in our bodies also affects how we feel emotionally, what we think, and how we react and relate to others. So, when we have that cold, we might feel emotionally numbed, and not able to enjoy things as before. You might find it harder to think things through, or make important decisions. If we were feeling ill like that, we might find we choose to wear different clothes at home, or eat or drink different foods. We also might relate to others differently - making sure that our illness is clearly communicated to them.

This illustrates an important point. That how we feel is affected by our bodies, thoughts and actions as well as what goes on around us.

This chapter will help you discover what makes you tick – and how you can gain a sense of control over how you feel and how you act. You can't change what you don't know- and by the end of this chapter you'll know a lot more about what makes you feel good – or bad.

Chapter 2

UNDERSTANDING YOUR FEELINGS

Too much
to do

SOMEONE CLOSE
IS REALLY ILL

Friends hate me

GOT
DUMPED

Best
friend
ignored
me

LOST
my job

Being
ill

Failed
the
exam

ALL
ALONE

Got
kicked
off the
team

GOT
CRITICISED

GOT NO
MONEY

BEING
BULLIED

No-one to talk to

You feel bad because you're in a vicious cycle

The way you feel is affected by things that happen to you. Like the things on the opposite page. Those things are all outside you. Sometimes, you can change what's happening outside, but often, you can't do much about them.

And when you allow them to affect your mood, a vicious cycle kicks in and you feel worse and worse and worse…

Vicious cycles spin by affecting five areas of your life.

Turn over to see how it works

First...
1. An outside event affects you

When something happens, you naturally notice it and think about it. If you forget your friend's birthday, for example, you may think "I'm a terrible friend!". This is called **Altered Thinking.**

Altered thinking can set off a chain reaction inside you that affects the way you feel and what you do.

When your altered thinking is negative (like "I'm a terrible friend"), the vicious cycle is triggered and you can end up really down, not getting out of bed and even feeling sick.

Let's see the Vicious Cycle in action

2. Altered thinking leads to...
3. Altered feelings

If you think "I'm a terrible friend!" you're going to feel pretty low, sad or guilty.

Maybe you feel as if you've let your friend down, or you might feel guilty because you know you could have been more organised.

So now what happens?

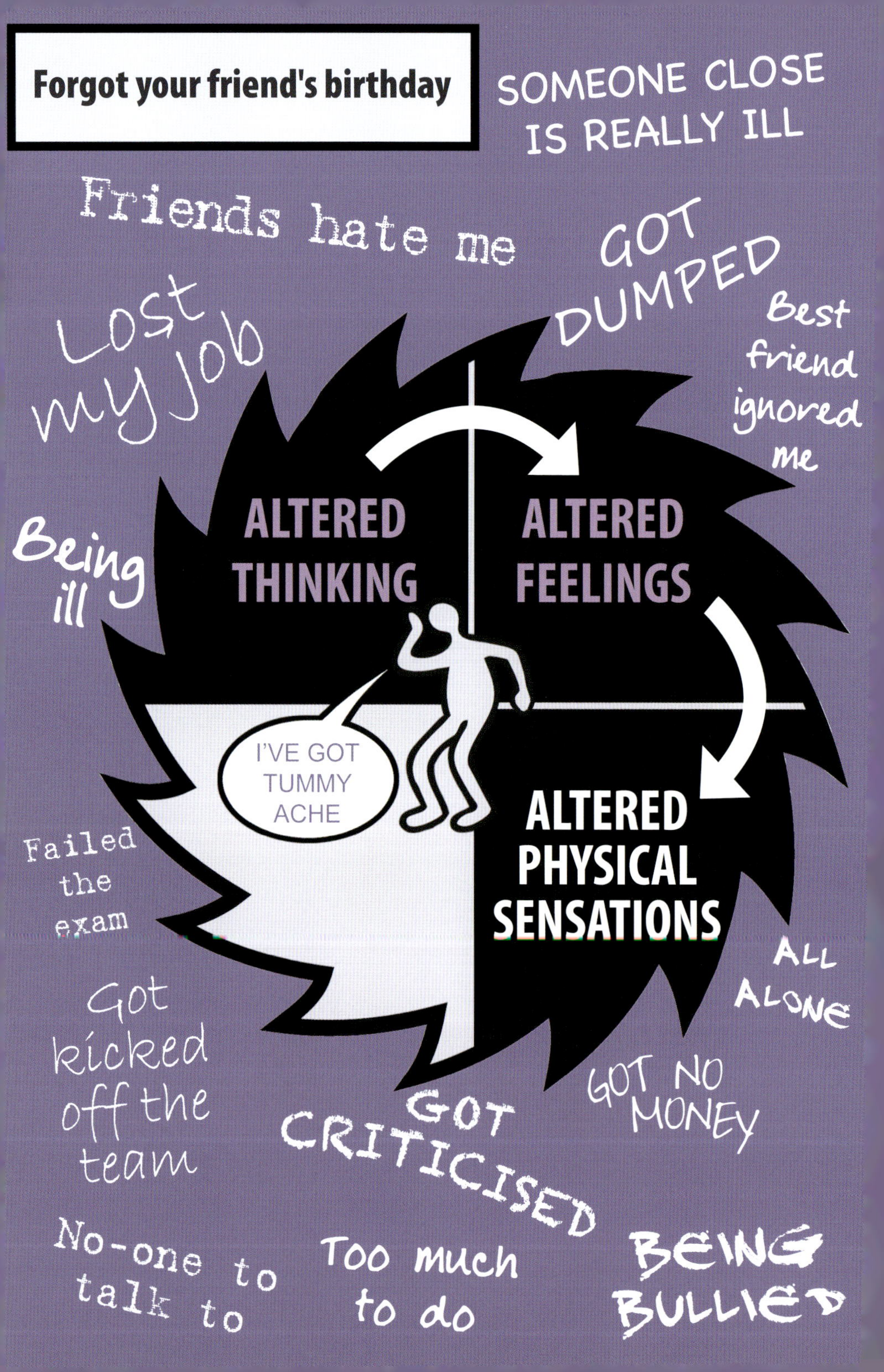
Forgot your friend's birthday
SOMEONE CLOSE IS REALLY ILL
Friends hate me
GOT DUMPED
Lost my job
Best friend ignored me
ALTERED THINKING
ALTERED FEELINGS
Being ill
I'VE GOT TUMMY ACHE
ALTERED PHYSICAL SENSATIONS
Failed the exam
ALL ALONE
Got kicked off the team
GOT NO MONEY
GOT CRITICISED
No-one to talk to
Too much to do
BEING BULLIED

Altered feelings lead to...
4. Altered physical sensations

When you feel low or guilty, you can get sweaty and tense and your stomach or your head can ache. Sometimes you can feel really tired.

Your hands might feel clammy, or you feel really tense and can't sit still.

Ever had a sinking feeling or felt your heart racing? It's probably that old vicious cycle spinning round!

What next?

Altered physical sensations lead to... 5. Altered behaviour

It's only natural. You're really tired, you have a headache or maybe feel tense, so you don't feel like going out, or even getting up. You steer clear of people who might ask if you sent a card or present. You stay in and hardly do any exercise. You're not eating right and you seem to catch all the bugs that are going round.

You even finish up at the doctor's, asking why you can't seem to shake off this virus you've had for weeks.

And you know what happens then? The cycle goes round again, only this time, you're already ill, staying in bed and fed up, so you get even worse.

Vicious, these cycles, aren't they? That's why it's important to work out how these five areas of life (outside events, thinking, feelings, physical sensations and behaviour) are affected by how you feel.

Now what about you?

COMPLETE YOUR OWN FIVE AREAS ASSESSMENT

You've read about how you might react if you missed your friend's birthday. Do you fall into other vicious cycles from time to time?

Here's how to play detective and work out how the vicious cycle affects you.

Choose a recent time when you felt bad. To start with, don't pick a time that is really upsetting or distressing. Instead choose a situation when you felt a bit down, fed up, angry, stressed, scared, frustrated, guilty, ashamed, tired, or in pain.

Now use the next two pages to work out how you reacted.

Pen at the ready?

Now's time to spot that vicious cycle!

MY FIVE AREAS ASSESSMENT

**living
life to
the full**
www.llttf.com

Understanding Feelings

Download from

www.llttf.com/resources

What's going on? Describe the situation:

My thoughts. Am I:

- Beating myself up?
- Focusing on the bad stuff?
- Being gloomy about the future?
- Expecting things to go wrong?
- Worrying what others may think about me?
- Other
  _____

My feelings. Do I feel:

- Low/Sad?
- Stressed/Anxious?
- Guilty?
- Ashamed?
- Angry/Irritable?
- Other
  _____

Altered Thinking

Altered Feelings

Altered Behaviour

Altered Physical Sensations

My behaviour. Am I choosing:

- Avoid something?
- Escape/Run away?
- Lean on others too much?
- Stop doing fun things?
- Stop seeing people I like?
- Doing things that can backfire?
- Other _____

My body. Am I:

- Shaky?
- Can't sleep?
- Heart racing?
- Dizzy?
- Other _____
- Tense?
- Sick?
- Off my food?
- Hot/Sweaty?
- Tired out?
- Cold/Clammy?
- Not able to relax?

Copyright Five Areas Resources Ltd (2021). Used under licence.
Download more for free from www.llttf.com/resources

61

YOUR VICIOUS CYCLE

Did you fall into a vicious cycle?

If you felt bad, it's likely the vicious cycle was spinning. What was the outside event - like a person or difficult situation? Did what you think affect how you felt - in your feelings and physical sensations? How did this affect what you did?

Did anything look familiar? Patterns of thinking, feeling or body reactions often repeat again and again. Did the cycle start to spin and make you feel even worse?

Stopping your cycle spinning takes practise. If you're feeling worse than usual it can feel hard to break the cycle.

Now for the *good* news!

YOU CAN STOP THE CYCLE!

You know the great thing about cycles?
They turn both ways!

In the same way that just one thing (an altered thought) led to everything else getting worse, you can start to make it better by changing one thing.

Just by acting differently, or changing the way you think about some things, you can affect **all the other things in the cycle** and start to feel better.

Sounds too easy? Turn over for an example.

How to stop the cycle

Example: The Cycle in action

1 **Situation:** You're walking down the street and someone you know walks by and doesn't say hello or smile.

2 **Altered thinking.** You jump to the conclusion they don't like you.

Oh no! She doesn't like me!

3 **Altered feelings.** This makes you feel bad.

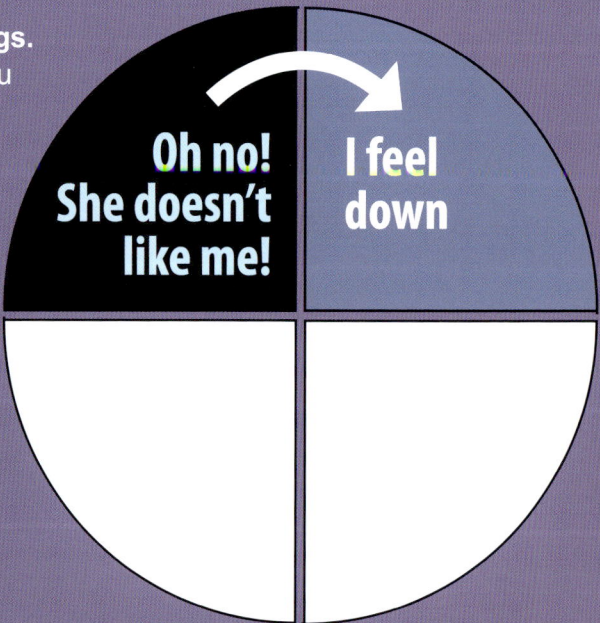

Oh no! She doesn't like me!

I feel down

4 **Altered physical sensations.** You have no energy and maybe can't sleep that night for worrying about what happened.

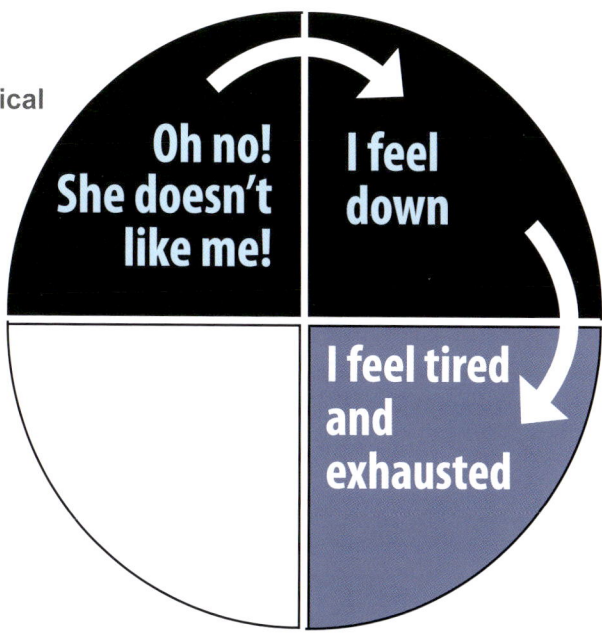

Oh no! She doesn't like me!

I feel down

I feel tired and exhausted

5 **Altered behaviour.** You go home and avoid other people's company.

Oh no! She doesn't like me!

I feel down

I stop seeing people

I feel tired and exhausted

and the Cycle spins....

Example: How to break the Cycle

1 **Situation:** You're walking down the street and someone you know walks by and doesn't say hello or smile.

2 **Altered thinking.** You look at things differently.

Poor Louise, she must be upset, I wonder what's wrong?

3 **Altered feelings.** You feel concerned and worried for Louise.

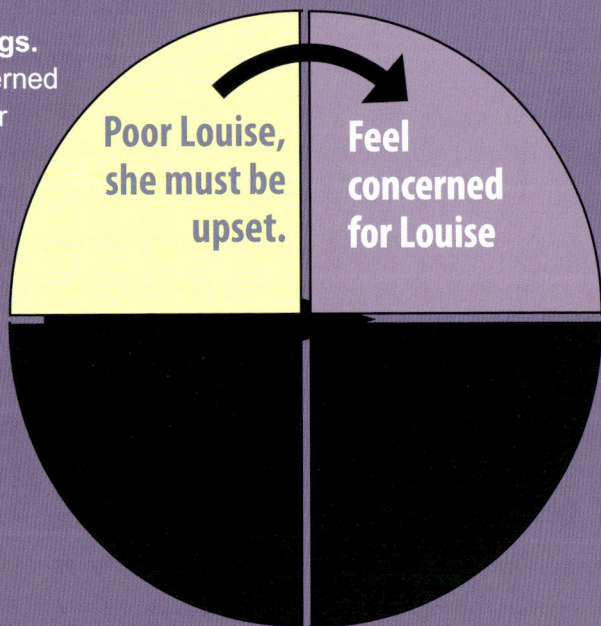

Poor Louise, she must be upset.

Feel concerned for Louise

4 **Altered physical sensations.** You feel energised to help.

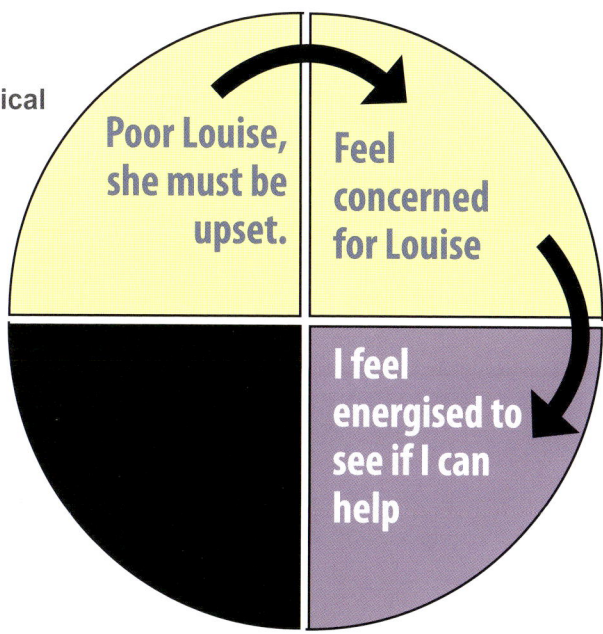

Poor Louise, she must be upset.

Feel concerned for Louise

I feel energised to see if I can help

5 **Altered behaviour.** You speak to Louise and enjoy it. She is worried about her mum. You arrange to meet up later.

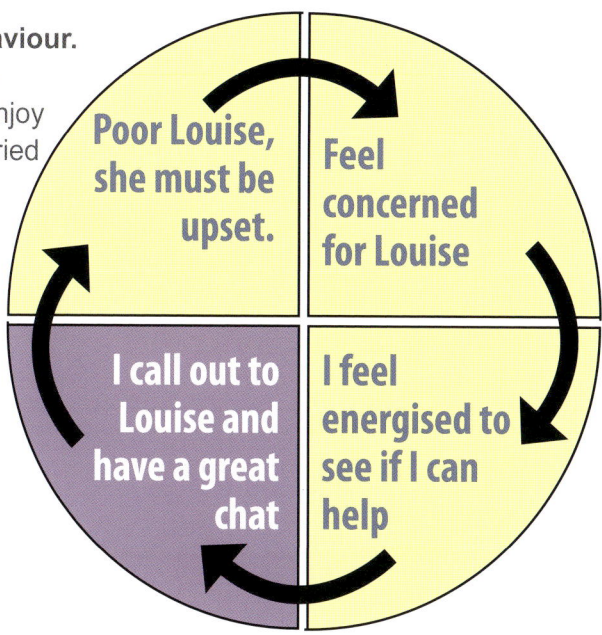

Poor Louise, she must be upset.

Feel concerned for Louise

I call out to Louise and have a great chat

I feel energised to see if I can help

YOU HAVE CONTROL

The cycle can come in any sequence of thoughts/feelings/bodily sensations and behaviour.

You can break the cycle by changing any of these areas.

You just need to change one thing

You can take control and stop the vicious cycle by changing just one thing – your thinking, your response, your activities – almost anything. And it doesn't have to be a big thing!

You could start by changing the way you react. By going out just one time. By doing just a bit more exercise. By changing the way you think about things.

If you manage to do something about just one thing, you'll break the vicious cycle, stop it spinning down and down and start to feel better straight away.

So here's what to do. Pick one small thing then use the Planner sheet on the next two pages to give yourself the best start.

Once you're done, use the Review sheet on the two pages after the Planner to check your progress.

Go, make a plan

Planner Sheet

Make a Plan!

1. What am I going to do?

Just one small thing

2. When am I going to do it?

That way you'll know if you don't do it

3. What problems or difficulties could happen, and how can I overcome them?

From the:
Living life to the full
resources.

Download from
www.llttf.com/resources

4. Is my planned task –

	Yes	No
• Useful for understanding or changing how I am?	☐	☐
• Specific, so that I will know when I have done it?	☐	☐
• Realistic, practical and achievable?	☐	☐

My notes:

Copyright Five Areas Resources Ltd (2021). Used under licence.
Download more for free from www.llttf.com/resources

LTTF

living
life to
the full
www.llttf.com

Review Sheet

How did it go? What did you plan to do?

Did you try to do it?   Yes ☐   No

If yes: What went well?

What didn't go so well?

What have you learned from what happened?

How are you going to apply what you have learned?

From the:
Living life to the full
resources.

Download from
www.llttf.com/resources

f no: What stopped you?

External things (other people, work or home issues etc.)

Internal things (forgot, not enough time, put it off, didn't think I could do it, couldn't see the point etc.)

ow can you tackle things differently next time?

Copyright Five Areas Resources Ltd (2021). Used under licence.
Download more for free from www.llttf.com/resources

NEXT STEPS

Use the five areas vicious cycle to make sense of why you feel the way you do. Remember, that's not all you've discovered. You've also learned some targets for change that will make a big difference.

What changes do you need to make in each of the five areas? When you've sorted your current problem, you might want to choose another area and work on something else in your life.

You can get added help and support at www.llttf.com - the award-winning web course. It's also the most recommended online resource for anxiety and depression by NHS England and widely recommended by charities, health and social care organisations.

Go for it!

Introduction to Chapter 3

Do you ever wake up in the morning and think - *"I just can't be bothered doing anything!"* You feel tired and not really wanting to do much at all. That feeling goes away when we get a few good night's sleep or when we slowly come around as the day continues. But what if that feeling sticks around far longer?

There's an important truth here - that the less we do, the less likely we are to do anything.

That's important because if we hit a rough patch and start to feel stressed, hassled or down, it can be so easy to feel overwhelmed and start to do less and less. We can withdraw from others, or take to our beds for longer. And a cycle can be set up where the less we do, the worse we feel, and the worse we feel, the less we do.

That's what this chapter focuses on. It will help you discover how you can improve how you feel by choosing to change what you do. It identifies the key ingredients for feeling good – having a daily routine that balances the *should* stuff and the *good* stuff. It helps you identify those good activities- the things you can do that will make you feel better.

Don't forget, you're in control.

Chapter 3

DOING THINGS THAT MAKE YOU FEEL BETTER

I feel too ill to do things

It's such a relief staying inside

I FEEL TIRED ALL THE TIME

I hardly see anyone these days

I don't even listen to music anymore

I DO WHAT I HAVE TO DO AND NO MORE

It's all too much effort

I haven't even got the energy to read this

I do things for everyone else but there's never any time for me

Know what? You're in a vicious cycle

When you feel low, you tend to stop doing things. You don't go out so much, you avoid seeing friends and you may even stop listening to music or watching sport.

As a result, you feel even lower, and then you feel like doing even less. It can seem such a relief to cut down and withdraw. It's tempting to take to bed, or sit or lie around all day. But if you do, you end up all seized up, feeling stiff, tired and overwhelmed.

It's like: the less you do, the worse you feel, the worse you feel, the less you do. And it keeps going round and round and round…

Things can get quite vicious.

SO, WHAT'S GOING ON?

living
life to
the full
www.llttf.com

Cycle of reduced activity

Download from

www.llttf.com/resources

1 Symptoms build.
Low, not sleeping/tired.
Scared, fed up.
Can't be bothered.

2 Everything seems harder.
Things seem pointless.
Not enjoyed.
Going through the motions.

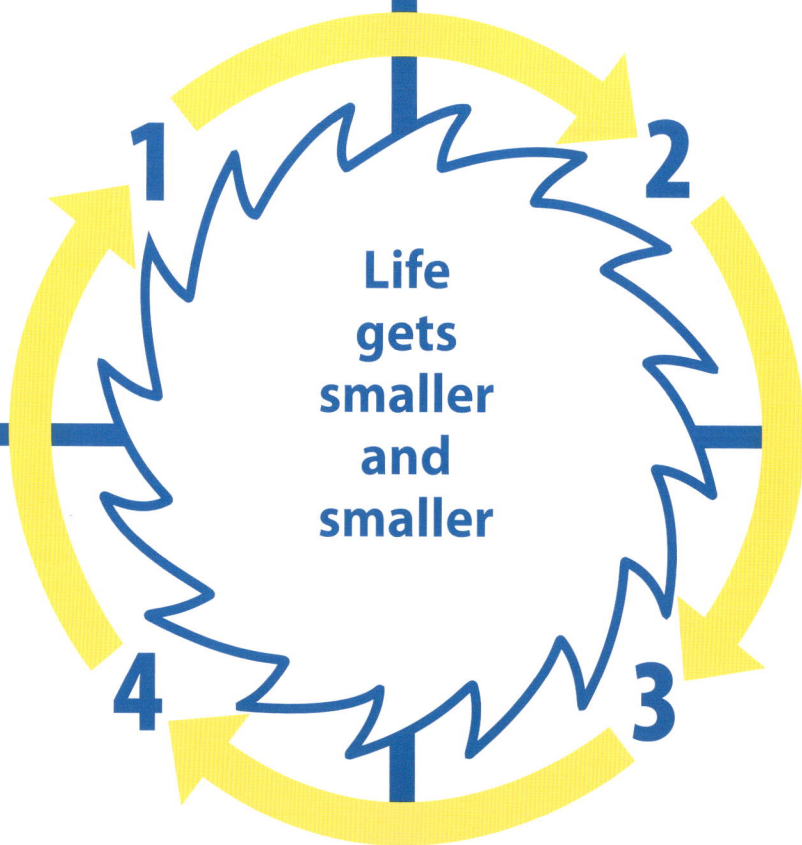

1

2

Life
gets
smaller
and
smaller

4

3

4 Count the cost.
Smaller life.
Feel worse and worse.
Lose confidence.

3 Cut down/avoid things that seem hard
Only do things you must/should do.
Less pleasure/achievement/closeness.

Copyright Five Areas Resources Ltd (2021). Used under licence.   83
Download more for free from www.llttf.com/resources

DO YOU KNOW WHAT YOU JUST DID?

VERY GOOD

You broke the cycle!

All it took was a little bit of positive action - turning that page.
Now all you have to do is take another tiny step, then another and another.
What steps? That's what this chapter is about – to show you the easy steps you can take to break that cycle into bits and start feeling better.

It involves making choices. Choosing to do things that make you feel better, rather than hiding away feeling worse and worse.

Important question coming up

WHAT DOES YOUR DAY LOOK LIKE?

When things seem hard, it's easy to lose your previous routine. It's tempting to lie in bed longer, stay up later, or have a longer nap when we can. But before you know it you lose the pattern and structure of your day and week.

What times do you typically get up?

… and go to bed?

These are the anchors that start and end your day. Other anchors that split your day are mealtimes. So, when do you eat?

Breakfast

Lunch

Your evening meal

If you skip any of these meals, leave the box blank.

Around these points are all the other activities of the day. Meeting friends, school work, household chores and more.

You need to get a routine going again. And start building in activities that you know are good for you.

First, look at what you do just now

Think about yesterday

Start by thinking about the last 24 hours. Write down everything you have done. Include things like getting dressed, watching TV, talking to a friend, going to school or college, washing your hair, etc. Then score them out of ten for pleasure, achievement and feeling close to other people. The first few spaces are filled in to show you how to do it. Doing this will help you understand what's good in your life and also to realise what's missing.

About closeness
Spending time with people you like is really important, but when we're down, we sometimes hide away. If your diary doesn't have enough things with a good closeness score, this chapter will help you sort that out.

	Pleasure	Getting things done	Closeness
Talking to my friend	9	3	10
Cleaning my room	1	10	0

	Pleasure	Getting things done	Closeness
_____	☐	☐	☐
_____	☐	☐	☐
_____	☐	☐	☐
_____	☐	☐	☐
_____	☐	☐	☐
_____	☐	☐	☐
_____	☐	☐	☐
_____	☐	☐	☐
_____	☐	☐	☐
_____	☐	☐	☐

Check your list and pick out the things you did that scored highly for pleasure, achievement or closeness to others. Write them down here.

Pleasure/fun: _____

Achievement/getting things done: _____

Closeness/people you like: _____

ANYTHING MISSING FROM YOUR DAY?

WHAT ABOUT THINGS YOU'VE STOPPED DOING?

Your day might not have contained all the things you like to do, so have a look through the list opposite and tick the one's that apply to you. Things you used to enjoy but haven't felt like doing lately.

Pleasure: what have you enjoyed?

- [ ] Enjoying sport.
- [ ] Listening to music.
- [ ] Watching a film.
- [ ] Going for a walk/Getting some fresh air.
- [ ] Playing a musical instrument.
- [ ] Reading a good book, magazine or blog.
- [ ] Practicing relaxation techniques.
- [ ] Cooking or baking for pleasure.

Achievement: Getting things done

- [ ] Pursuing a hobby.
- [ ] Gardening/looking after plants.
- [ ] Doing exercise.
- [ ] Doing drama.
- [ ] Cleaning a room/doing household chores.

Closeness: have you spent time with people you like?

- [ ] Seeing your friends.
- [ ] Watching TV with a friend.
- [ ] Phoning or texting friends.
- [ ] Going to a class or club.
- [ ] Going to church, mosque, temple or synagogue.
- [ ] Spending time with family.
- [ ] Helping other people.

Well ticked!

Now choose an activity you want to do

USE WHAT YOU'VE FOUND TO START FILLING YOUR DAY WITH GOOD STUFF

Remember, the things that make you smile.

One of the reasons we feel worse when we stop doing things, is the fact that it's usually the things we like that we cut down on first.
No wonder life seems to go down and down!

To start it going up again, you need to pick good things to fill your day with. Not all the time – just one thing to start with. So, the next step of your plan is to look at the lists you just made and pick one of the things on them.

Pick something that used to give you pleasure, or a sense of achievement/getting things done. Or something that you think is worthwhile or made you feel close to others.

Just one thing to start with.

An activity you value and see as important to your life.

NOW WRITE IT HERE SO YOU DON'T FORGET IT.

_____

_____

_____

_____

GOOD

You've just written down the thing you're going to start doing again. Something worth getting up for.

Now, you're going to do it

NOW PLAN WHEN YOU'LL DO IT

Say what and when

Think about the activity you want to do first.

Write down *what* you will do, and *when* you will do it into the Activity Planner on the next two pages.

Just now it will stand out as the only activity there.

Go, ahead, write it in.

You don't want it to feel lonely, so soon you'll be adding other activities into the Activity Planner.

But to start with just include:
- The single activity you planned - the one you wrote down two pages ago.
- Next, add your daily anchors: the meals you have through the day, and the times you get up and go to bed.

There's plenty of time to add more activities, but for now just focus on the first activity you're going to do.

MY ACTIVITY PLANNER

Plan a balance of activities over the days and week.

Get into a routine - a time to get up, eat, go to school, go to bed, and do any work or chores, or perhaps to go for a walk, meet friends or attend after school activities.

Choose things you value and see as important, things that give a sense of Pleasure, Achievement or Closeness.

Plan in the key essentials that otherwise will build up and cause you problems - paying bills, cutting the lawn, doing the washing-up, ironing, having a haircut etc.

The plan is to build what you do up over a few weeks so you end up with one activity planned in each part of the day. Leave some gaps for the unexpected things that crop up. Also, allow some time just for you.

My activity planner

Download from
www.llttf.com/resources

	Morning	Afternoon	Evening
Monday			
Tuesday			
Wednesday			
Thursday			
Friday			
Saturday			
Sunday			

Now build on it

Copyright Five Areas Resources Ltd (2021). Used under licence.
Download more for free from www.llttf.com/resources

REMEMBER THAT LONELY ACTIVITY?

Now let's give it some friends

Rebuild your routine

Having to get out of bed to walk the dog or get ready for school or college can be a real pain, especially on cold mornings, but it's also a great way to feel better. No dog? Then make yourself a routine with other things. Getting up and showering. Eating breakfast. Playing your music. Getting on the bus. Cleaning the house. Can't get out? Make the most of activities you can do.

And if you rebuild your routine with things that involve others (messaging someone you like after school, walking to school with a friend) you'll feel even better because of that closeness thing we mentioned before.

That's because the more of the right stuff you do, the better you feel, and the better you feel, the more you want to do things. Add these to your Activity Planner.

More good stuff on the next page

ADD SOME MORE OF THE GOOD STUFF

Plan a series of other activities, then add them one by one into your Activity Planner. Make each activity small and not too difficult. Don't be too ambitious, be easy on yourself. And don't worry if you have to keep crossing things out, there's plenty of space.

- Choose some of the good stuff that helps how you feel.

- Add in some of the things you've cut down or stopped doing that used to be good too.

- Choose things you value and give a sense of pleasure, achievement or closeness.

- Build things up over a few weeks so you end up with one activity planned in each part of the day.

With each activity you add, you're breaking that vicious cycle, and making it spin the other way so you feel better and better.

Are you ignoring important things?

Some activities may seem hard or boring. Paying for clothes, looking after yourself, keeping up with course work - they can all seem too much trouble when you're feeling down.

The problem is some activities are necessary, and if you don't do them it makes you feel worse and can leave you in a mess. So here's what to do: choose one thing that wasn't in your diary but should have been, and plan to do it - now.

Write that essay. Make that call. Get your hair done. Do some tidying. Wash the dishes.

You'll feel loads better afterwards and you'll be able to add it to your diary and put a 10 in the 'achievement' box!

Aim for the following

You know what makes you feel good.

Across each day and week you need to get a mix of those activities that help.

Start with the things you can change most easily. Aim for variety so you address each of the key areas:

1. Pleasure: things that make you feel good.
2. Achievement: things you value and see as important.
3. Closeness: where you connect with people you like or are important to you.
4. Finally don't forget to do things that are important and necessary.

Each of these activities breaks the vicious cycle and makes you feel better.
But don't rush. Some activities need to be built up to slowly.

TAKING STEPS THAT MOVE YOU FORWARDS

Some activities may be good for you, but seem just too hard to do all at once. You need to work up to doing them step by step.

How?

Have a look at the example opposite.

For example:

Jack used to like meeting his friends for a walk in the park, but since he's been feeling low he hasn't had the energy for it. This is what he wrote in his plan for getting back to meeting them.

Step 1. Go to the park and just sit there enjoying the peace and quiet.

Step 2. Go back to the park and walk by myself. Don't need to talk to anyone if I don't feel like it.

Step 3. Get into the habit of walking by myself 2 or 3 times a week.

Step 4. Get in touch with one friend and arrange to have a walk and a chat.

Step 5. Go to the park with my friend at a time when we're likely to see the others.

Step 6. Arrange to meet the others next time they're walking in the park.

Step 7. Keep going – get into a routine and feel the difference!

Jack knew he could take one step a day, or one step a week, it didn't matter. What mattered was having a plan and making steady progress towards getting some fun back in his life.

Right, that's enough of Jack. Now back to your plan.

105

WRITE DOWN AN ACTIVITY THAT YOU NEED TO BUILD UP TO STEP BY STEP HERE

Now think about the little steps you can take towards doing it. Don't be overly ambitious, be easy on yourself. And don't worry if you have to keep crossing things out, there's plenty of space.

1. I'm going to _____

2. Then I'm going to _____

3. Next, I'm going to _____

4. Then I'm going to _____

5. _____

6. _____

7. _____

8. _____

SOUNDS EASY DOESN'T IT?

But you know change sometimes isn't that easy

Remember all those failed New Year's resolutions? Promises to change that seem hard? Or maybe we forget, or find we can't be bothered, or talk ourselves out of things?

So, let's recognise something. It's hard to make changes. That's why we've asked you to pick activities to do that you know can be good for you.

But if you find you get stuck doing a particular activity, here's a helping hand to make a plan to do it that will work.

Turn over to make your plan

Planner Sheet

Make a Plan!

1. What am I going to do?

Just one small thing

2. When am I going to do it?

That way you'll know if you don't do it

3. What problems or difficulties could happen, and how can I overcome them?

From the:
Living life to the full resources.

Download from
www.llttf.com/resources

4. Is my planned task –

	Yes	No
• Useful for understanding or changing how I am?		
• Specific, so that I will know when I have done it?		
• Realistic, practical and achievable?		

My notes:

Copyright Five Areas Resources Ltd (2021). Used under licence.
Download more for free from www.llttf.com/resources

HOW
DID
IT GO?

Life's all about learning

If you make a plan and everything goes smoothly- that's great!

But you can also learn a lot from when things go wrong too. So, if there are problems with your plan- that's great too. It's great because you can play detective and learn.
So, if you got stuck, or something was difficult, ask yourself some questions. Was the problem something *internal* – inside you (like forgetting, or you couldn't be bothered), or *external* – for example a problem caused by someone else, the weather, or unexpected circumstances? Use whatever you discover to make your next plan even better.

You'll find a useful Review sheet to help you with this learning on the next two pages.
Try to get into a sequence of *Plan* (using the Planner sheet), *Do*, and *Review* (using the Review sheet) for whenever you are planning more difficult activities. That way you will keep moving forwards.

Review Sheet

How did it go? What did you plan to do?

Did you try to do it?

Yes ☐   No ☐

If yes: What went well?

What didn't go so well?

What have you learned from what happened?

How are you going to apply what you have learned?

114

From the:
Living life to the full
resources.

Download from

www.llttf.com/resources

If no: What stopped you?

External things (other people, work or home issues etc.)

Internal things (forgot, not enough time, put it off, didn't think I could do it, couldn't see the point etc.)

How can you tackle things differently next time?

Copyright Five Areas Resources Ltd (2021). Used under licence.
Download more for free from www.llttf.com/resources

WHAT IF SOMETHING GOT IN YOUR WAY?

Learn from it. So as soon as you've written your next plan, think about what could stop it happening. Are you planning to change too much too quickly? Are there things that might trip you up? What about other people? Could someone be unhelpful at any stage?

When you've figured out what could block your progress, work out another mini-plan for getting around the obstacle. It's called unblocking.

Things to watch out for

Don't try and make every change possible all at once.

Be realistic – you're planning for success not a let-down. You know your own personality and how inpatient or ambitious you are. That's where it's important to be wise and plan just one main change a day to start with.

So, pick just a few things to get you started, and make a separate plan to do each using the Planner sheet. Then plan them in across the day and the week using the Activity Planner.

1. Leave some gaps for the unexpected things that crop up.
2. Include some time just for you.
3. Remember the anchors - a time to get up, eat, go to bed.
4. Add in some more routines like a regular time to do the household chores, or perhaps to go for a walk, meet friends or attend a regular class.
5. Make sure your plan fits with your values/ideals of how you want to live.

But don't forget that some things are important to do even if they aren't much fun or seem difficult.

AT THE END OF EACH DAY

Create a Happy List to help you remember

Each evening, sit down and write down three things that you:

- Have enjoyed.
- Felt was a job well done (achievement).
- Or helped you feel close to someone.

What are you thankful for?

After a few days, you'll have a list of great things that you can look back on. It will help you remember how you're changing things.

Time to give yourself a pat on the back and say well done!

Now, keep going with more plans until you get a good balance of activities across the day and the week. You'll feel the difference!

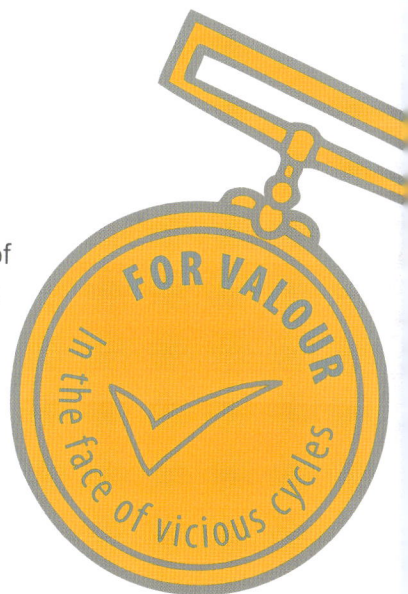

FOR VALOUR

In the face of vicious cycles

Go for it!

Introduction to Chapter 4

Have you ever looked through a Kaleidoscope? Everything seems beautiful and colourful. The red, green, yellow and blue shapes form in fantastic combinations and draw your attention.

How we think can be like that. We can choose to focus on the amazing, the good things, the people around us we like and who like us, the places we love and the hobbies and interests we enjoy.

But sometimes it can seem the opposite happens. We become focused on the difficulties - the challenges and the hard things in life. We may notice the things we haven't done more than the things we have done. We pick over our faults and weaknesses rather than celebrate the good things in our lives.

In this chapter you'll discover what Unhelpful thoughts are and what they look like. Unhelpful thoughts are thoughts that make us feel worse, in our feelings, bodies or relationships. Like celebrities they crave attention and always like to be in the spotlight. But maybe not everything they say is always true, helpful or accurate.

At times when we feel under pressure Unhelpful thoughts pop into our minds more, and are harder to shift. They become a focus and start to make us feel even more stressed, down or emotional. Together they also cause us to react in ways that make things worse such as withdrawing from others, or doing things that can backfire on how we feel.

You'll learn some effective ways of relating differently to these upsetting thoughts. This chapter will help you play detective, spot thoughts that have a bad impact on us, and put them in their place.

Remember, you have control.

Chapter 4

LOOKING AT THINGS DIFFERENTLY

Everyone thinks I'm a loser

Nobody likes me

I ALWAYS MESS UP

IF I DON'T GET THIS SORTED OUT - I WON'T COPE

WHAT'S THE POINT?

THINGS NEVER WORK OUT FOR ME

It's all my fault

Sound familiar?

That's because loads of people think that way - but when you're already feeling pretty bad, thoughts like these make you feel even worse.

The fact is, certain thoughts **cause** bad feelings. It's not just the other way round. So one way to feel better is to respond differently to upsetting thoughts.

This chapter will show you how.

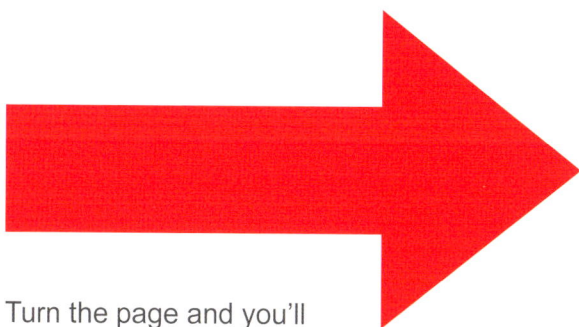

Turn the page and you'll see what we mean.

GOOD MOVE!

You turned the page!

You didn't say "Oh, forget it!" and chuck the book out of the window. You turned the page and took a giant leap towards feeling better - by yourself.

Keep on turning and you'll find out how to *keep on* feeling better and better, with the

Amazing Unhelpful Thought Busting Programme

Now you're going to learn to spot some unhelpful thoughts.

LET'S PLAY DETECTIVE

Magnifying Glass at the ready?

The key to good detective work is to slow things down and be on the lookout.

Try this task to start noticing your own unhelpful thoughts.

Imagine yourself into each situation, and try to spot the thoughts that pop into your mind.

1). You're late for an important exam. You're stuck in traffic and can see the building you want to reach. You know you're going to be really late.

2). You invite friends round to watch a movie, but notice one of them looks bored.

3). You play sport but this week you're not picked to play.

Then complete the worksheet on the next two pages. Use the questions to help you identify the thoughts that occur. Write down as many as you notice, then turn the page to label the thoughts.

My Unhelpful Thoughts

How to notice thoughts that have a bad impact on how you feel and what you do.

Choose a time when you felt worse. What went through your mind at the time?

- About what you've done or not done?
- About you?
- About others?
- About what has happened?
- About what might happen?
- About what others think about you?
- Any pictures or images that come into your mind?

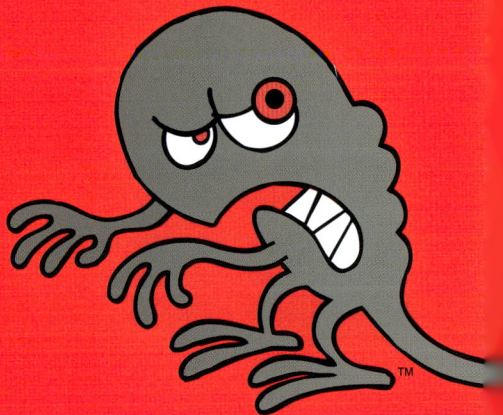

LLTTF and the Bad thought bug image are registered trademarks of Five Areas Resources Ltd.

From the:
Living life to the full
resources.

Download from

www.llttf.com/resources

My Unhelpful Thoughts

Copyright Five Areas Resources Ltd (2021). Used under licence.
Download more for free from www.llttf.com/resources.

Unhelpful Thinking Styles

Are any of these thinking styles familiar?

Have you been here before?

If you tick one or more boxes you've spotted an unhelpful thought that you can aim to change.

Are you your own worst critic?

Do you always seem to be beating yourself up about something?

☐

Do you focus on the bad stuff?

As if you were looking at the world through darkened glasses?

☐

Do you have a gloomy view of the future?

Expecting everything to turn out badly?

☐

From the:
Living life to the full
resources.

Download from

www.llttf.com/resources

Are you jumping to the worst conclusions?

Thinking it's the end of the world.

Do you assume that others see you badly?

When you haven't checked whether it's true, it's called 'Mind Reading'

Do you take responsibility for everything?

Including things that aren't your fault?

Are you always saying things like 'should' and 'got to'?

Setting impossible standards for yourself?

Turn the page to respond differently

Copyright Five Areas Resources Ltd (2021). Used under licence.
Download more for free from www.llttf.com/resources.

The Amazing Unhelpful Thought Busting Programme

Step 1

First, label the thought

When you notice an unhelpful thought that has a bad impact on how you feel or what you do, don't get caught up in it. Instead, just mentally step back and stick a label on it.

"Oh that's just one of those unhelpful thoughts".

When you label an unhelpful thought this way, **it** loses its power and **you** realise it's just part of being upset.

It's not the truth, it's just one of those unhelpful thoughts.

You could even talk to it. Say: "You're spotted! I'm not playing that game again!"

Turn over for **Step 2**

133

The Amazing Unhelpful Thought Busting Programme

Step 2

NOW LEAVE IT ALONE

Mentally turn your back on the thought. Don't challenge it or try to argue with it, just let it be.

Unhelpful thoughts love attention so don't give them any.

Instead, think about what you're doing right now, or stuff that you're planning for the future, or things you've achieved lately.

Unhelpful Thought ©

Step 3 next

Step 3

STAND UP TO IT!

Don't be bossed about by unhelpful thoughts

Unhelpful thoughts can be intimidating. But although they sound strong, really they're weak underneath. And they tell lies.

They say you won't like doing something. They say you'll fail if you try. They tell you you're rubbish or you're scared or nobody likes you.

Just because the thought claims something doesn't mean it's true.

Act against it and test it out!
If the thought says "Don't" then DO!
If the thought says "Can't" say "CAN!"
Right back at it.

Easy for us to say? You're right.

But if you don't give it a try you'll never know.

Turn over for the next step

137

The Amazing Unhelpful Thought Busting Programme

Step 4

GIVE YOURSELF A BREAK

Be a better friend to yourself, you deserve it

Unhelpful thoughts are how we beat ourselves up when we're upset. We often say things to ourselves that are critical and nasty – things we would never say to someone we cared for. And we often say things to ourselves in such a nasty or scary tone.

So, if you're having trouble with an upsetting thought, think what a person who really loved and wanted the best for you would say. What words of encouragement and support might they offer?

They'd disagree with the unhelpful thoughts. They'd remind you that you're not rubbish, or stupid, or bound to fail.

Trust these compassionate words and let them help you get rid of the unhelpful thoughts.

BE KIND

Turn over for **Step 5**

139

Step 5

HOW TO BEAT THE REALLY DIFFICULT ONES

Some unhelpful thoughts are hard to beat.

They keep coming back and you wonder if you'll ever get the better of them.

Here are some things you can do that will help.

Look at the situation differently

First, imagine what it would be like if it was a friend, not you, who was having this thought. What advice would you give? Now give the same advice to yourself.

Put your thought or worry into perspective. Will it matter in six weeks or six months? Will you even remember what the problem was? If it won't matter then, it's probably not that important now.

How would others you trust and respect deal with the problem? Think about someone who seems to handle problems well and work out what they would do, or how they would think in this situation.

Are you basing this on how you feel rather than the facts.

Really Unhelpful Thought

Finally, consider if you are looking at the whole picture.

Turn over to RECAP

The Amazing Unhelpful Thought Busting Programme

Recap

SO:

The Amazing Unhelpful Thought Busting Programme

Unhelpful thoughts mess you up and actually **cause** bad feelings. Beat those thoughts and you'll feel better. When you notice an upsetting thought:

1. LABEL IT

Oh, you're just one of those unhelpful thoughts.

2. LEAVE IT

Unhelpful thoughts need attention, so don't give them any.

3. STAND UP TO IT

Unhelpful thoughts can be scary and intimidating, but tell lies. You can beat them.

4. GIVE YOURSELF A BREAK

What would someone who really loved you say? Trust them and let them help you beat the unhelpful thought.

5. LOOK AT IT DIFFERENTLY

Give yourself the advice you'd give to a friend. Ask yourself if it will matter in days or six weeks. Pick someone you trust and respect and work out how they would handle the situation.

Reflect on which approach works best for you.

So what are you waiting for? Let's try it out

living life to the full
LTTF™
www.llttf.com

The Amazing Unhelpful Thought Busting Programme

To deal with upsetting thoughts you need to choose to respond differently. Try each of the following approaches and discover which ones work for you.

1 Label it

- Oh, you're just one of those unhelpful thoughts.

2 Leave it

- Unhelpful thoughts often demand attention. Let them be.

3 Stand up to it

- Unhelpful thoughts can be intimidating. You can beat them.

From the:
Living life to the full
resources.

Download from

www.llttf.com/resources

4 Be kind to yourself: Give yourself a break

- What warm words of encouragement would someone say?
  Say them to yourself.

5 Look at it differently

- Give yourself the advice you'd give a friend.

- Ask yourself if it will matter in six weeks or months?

- What would other people you trust and respect say?

- Are you basing this on how you feel rather than the facts.

- Are you looking at the whole picture?

Copyright Five Areas Resources Ltd (2007-2021). Used under licence.
Download more for free from www.llttf.com/resources.

GO FOR IT!

Don't worry

... if this seems hard at first. A good place to start is to practice on unhelpful thoughts that are only slightly upsetting to begin with.

It takes practice to beat upsetting thoughts.

But the Amazing Unhelpful Thought Busting Program really works, so keep trying and within a few days, you'll have your unhelpful thoughts on the run and be feeling better.

Remember the key thing is to plan to practice this approach.

Use the Planner sheet on the next two pages to create a good plan. Then review how it went using the Review sheet on the two pages immediately after the Planner sheet.

Go for it!

Planner Sheet

Make a Plan!

1. What am I going to do?

Just one small thing

2. When am I going to do it?

That way you'll know if you don't do it

3. What problems or difficulties could happen, and how can I overcome them?

From the:
Living life to the full
resources.

Download from

www.llttf.com/resources

4. Is my planned task –

	Yes	No
• Useful for understanding or changing how I am?	☐	☐
• Specific, so that I will know when I have done it?	☐	☐
• Realistic, practical and achievable?	☐	☐

My notes:

Copyright Five Areas Resources Ltd (2007-2021). Used under licence.
Download more for free from www.llttf.com/resources.

living life to the full
www.llttf.com

Review Sheet

How did it go? What did you plan to do?

Did you try to do it?   Yes ☐   No ☐

If yes: What went well?

What didn't go so well?

What have you learned from what happened?

How are you going to apply what you have learned?

From the:
Living life to the full
resources.

Download from

www.llttf.com/resources

f no: What stopped you?

External things (other people, work or home issues etc.)

Internal things (forgot, not enough time, put it off, didn't think I could do it, couldn't see the point etc.)

ow can you tackle things differently next time?

Copyright Five Areas Resources Ltd (2021). Used under licence.
Download more for free from www.llttf.com/resources

Introduction to Chapter 5

Most of us can tackle problems most of the time. But if there are too many challenges that we face all at once, or if the problems seem huge and overwhelming, then most of us can start to feel the pressure and begin to feel out of control.

It's so easy when we feel there's too much being demanded to feel daunted. We look at the amount of information to revise, or the mountain of other demands we face and feel stuck, not knowing how to even start.

There's an added difficulty. At times when we feel stressed or down, we can find it difficult coming up with possible plans to sort out the problem. Even if we can come up with some solutions, if we feel stressed it's more likely we'll dismiss each possible response as not being likely to work.

The result is we feel trapped as if we are in a one way street and can't get out. All we focus on is the problem and our sense of powerlessness. So, what do we need to do? Just like that blind alley or a dead end you need to stop, look around and get clear where you are, then figure out how to plan your way out of there.

In this chapter you will learn an approach that you can use to tackle any problem. Yes, really, any problem. Whether you want to save or make some money, complete a project at home, tackle your step-brother or sister who is playing their music too loud when you're trying to sleep or even learn to play the guitar!

Remember, when it comes to problems, you'll learn a fresh and effective plan you can use.

Chapter 5

HOW TO FIX ALMOST EVERYTHING

IN

4 EASY STEPS

(A GUIDE TO PRACTICAL PROBLEM SOLVING)

Finish a project

Eat
healthily

GET A JOB

SPEND
WISELY

Get fitter

Revise for exams

GET
ACTIVE

Make more
friends

Plan for a
holiday

get out
more

Yes, almost everything

It doesn't matter what you want to do, this Easy 4-Step Plan will help you do it.

It works particularly well if you're feeling you don't know where to start. In fact it works even if you're so fed up you can only just be bothered reading this page.

The idea is to break your big problems or goal into tiny little steps that by themselves are easy to do.

Then you work out how you're going to do each step, make a plan, and carry it out. It's called the Easy 4-Step Plan.

To get to the top of an enormous climbing wall:

a. Break the climb into small steps

b. Take it one step at a time

Turn over
for **STEP 1**

OVERWHELMED BY PROBLEMS?

CHOOSE A SINGLE SMALL GOAL

When you have too many problems or a single big problem- where do you even start?

No friends? Can't get through all your homework? Feeling overwhelmed by problems that look huge? When you break them into smaller steps, they're less intimidating and a lot easier to fix. Tackling a problem is like climbing a wall. That's why step 1 of the E4SP is 'choose a single smaller goal'.

Let's say you feel you never see your friends. You could break the week into bits and make an effort to see friends on Mondays, for example.

If you think you are spending too much time alone you could try watching TV with someone a couple of nights a week instead of sitting in your room. Why not phone your friends and have a conversation rather than texting?

Or if you feel you're on social media or watching TV too much, you could start by not doing it for an afternoon or a day. Most problems can be chopped up like this, and you're much more likely to succeed when you do things bit by bit.

The key is choosing a realistic goal that will make a real difference, but isn't too big that it seems impossible.

Turn over for **STEP 2**

THINK OF CREATIVE WAYS TO TACKLE THE FIRST STEP

Grab a piece
of paper...

And write down all the things you could do to work on the first bit of the problem.

The trick with being creative is to let your mind run free, and write everything down - the wacky things as well as the sensible ones.

To start seeing more of your friends, you could join an after school club that is held every Monday.

Spending too much time watching TV? You could get out one of those board games you like to play at holiday time. Or ask a friend to play sport. Or choose to chat about people's days as you eat in the evening.

Trying to cut down on social media or apps? Leave your phone in another room. Or put it on silent for part of the day. Switch it off at a certain time in the evening.

If you write everything down, there's bound to be a good idea in there somewhere.

STEP 3 next

CHOOSE AN IDEA AND MAKE A PLAN TO DO IT

Step by step

Look at your list of creative ideas and pick one. Choose one that looks do-able and doesn't scare you too much.
Now take another piece of paper and write down, step by step, how to actually DO it.

Make the steps as small as you like: Get up. Get dressed. Walk to front door. Open door…. and so on.

OR

To see friends more: text a friend, look at activities you could do together, sign up for the after school club, invite someone to your new favourite coffee shop….like that.

OR

For using social media less: leave your phone in the other room, forget your phone on purpose one day when you go out, set your phone and computer up to block some social media sites. Make sure that the steps are small, straightforward and seem like things you could really do.

What if something gets in the way?

As soon as you've written your plan, think about what could stop it happening. Are there any unforeseen events that might trip you up? What about other people? Could someone be unhelpful at any stage?

When you've figured out what might block your progress, work out another mini-plan for getting round the obstacle.

Final step coming up

This way, you'll be ready for whatever happens!

CHECK THE PLAN AND PUT IT INTO ACTION

This is it! You've written down all the steps, now you need to check that they're do-able. Use this checklist:

Is it just one thing? ☐
You're not planning to change everything all at once.

Are you aiming at just one thing? ☐
Don't try and do more than one item on your list at the same time. You can always pick another when you've sorted the first one.

Is it slow? ☐
There's no need to rush at things. Your plan can take as long as you like, so long as you stick to it, step by step.

Is it easy? ☐
Make your steps small and easy and you'll be more likely to do them.

Are you ready to unblock it? ☐
Have you thought about what could go wrong and how to deal with it?

FIVE TICKS?

THEN GO FOR IT!

Still a bit doubtful?

THAT'S EASY FOR YOU TO SAY!

Don't worry, you can do it

The Easy 4-Step Plan really works, even when you have a really tough problem to deal with.

Remember the climbing wall - you can get to the top step by step. All you have to do is keep on climbing!

And don't be too hard on yourself if things don't go so smoothly half way through. Just calmly go back to the plan and take those small, steady steps again.

But what about when your enthusiasm goes? When the novelty wears off and you can't remember why you went to all this trouble in the first place?

That's when you need the next two pages!

Easy 4-Step Plan

1 Choose a single small goal

If you're facing lots of problem - pick just one to work on at first.
Write it here:

Will changing it have a helpful impact on how you feel, or on your situation?

2 Think of creative ways to tackle the first step

From the:
Living life to the full
resources.

Download from

www.llttf.com/resources

3 Choose an idea and make a plan to do it

Not too large a step so it's unrealistic - or too small so that it doesn't address the problem.

4 Check the plan and put it into action

- [ ] Are you aiming at just one thing?

- [ ] Is it realistic?

- [ ] Is it slow enough?

- [ ] Is it easy - not too big?

- [ ] Are you ready to unblock it?

Copyright Five Areas Resources Ltd (2021). Used under licence.
Download more for free from www.llttf.com/resources.

NOW DO IT

TRY OUT YOUR PLAN

Moving forward bit by bit

Now you have used the Easy 4-Step Plan to plan the first change, you need to carry out your plan. Sounds easy? But we all know sometimes we can get stuck or derailed. We may lose motivation, talk ourselves out of it, or maybe things change and the initial plan needs changing. Or we forget.

That's where making a clear plan to put what you've learned into action can help. The Planner sheet on the next two pages can really help. It helps provide a double check on your plan - and also forces you to be clear exactly what you are going to do and when you are going to do it. Once you've done that, use the Review sheet that follows to learn from how things went.

Remember to work on your problem bit by bit using the Easy 4-Step and Planner/ Review sheets to plan each step one at a time (remember that climbing wall!). You can download more worksheets for free from www.llttf.com/resources

Planner Sheet

Make a Plan!

1. What am I going to do?

Just one small thing

2. When am I going to do it?

That way you'll know if you don't do it

3. What problems or difficulties could happen, and how can I overcome them?

From the:
Living life to the full resources.

Download from
www.llttf.com/resources

4. Is my planned task -

	Yes	No
• Useful for understanding or changing how I am?	☐	☐
• Specific, so that I will know when I have done it?	☐	☐
• Realistic, practical and achievable?	☐	☐

My notes:

Copyright Five Areas Resources Ltd (2021). Used under licence.
Download more for free from www.llttf.com/resources.

living
life to
the full
www.llttf.com

Review Sheet

How did it go? What did you plan to do?

Did you try to do it?   Yes ☐   No ☐

If yes: What went well?

What didn't go so well?

What have you learned from what happened?

How are you going to apply what you have learned?

From the:
**Living life to the full
resources.**

Download from
www.llttf.com/resources

f no: What stopped you?

External things (other people, work or home issues etc.)

Internal things (forgot, not enough time, put it off, didn't think I could do it, couldn't see the point etc.)

low can you tackle things differently next time?

Copyright Five Areas Resources Ltd (2021). Used under licence.
Download more for free from www.llttf.com/resources

WHAT TO DO WHEN THE GOING GETS TOUGH

Remind yourself why you're doing this

If you're having trouble keeping going, say, in the middle of your plan when things are getting difficult, try these ideas to remind yourself why you started in the first place.

- Write down the reasons you want to do this and put them where you can see them.
- Think about how you'll be in 2 or 3 years time if you give in now. Write that down and place your list where you can see it to motivate you.
- Think about the advantages of succeeding – better health, better relationships, passing that exam, having more friends, having more fun, having more money, doing better overall. Again, write them down and put them where you can see them.
- Tell as many people as possible what you're doing, so that they can help you (or remind you when you find things difficult).

Ready for some real-life examples?

If you're not sure how to apply the plan to your problem, the next few pages will help. They're full of real plans showing how people like you have fixed different things and turned their lives around.

How the **Easy 4-Step Plan** works in real life

I WANT TO MAKE NEW FRIENDS

Step 1: Choose a single small goal

How do you break a bigger general problem like 'making new friends' into little steps? Change it to 'make *one* new friend'. It's a lot easier to work at finding and connecting with one person than to try to transform yourself into the life and soul of the neighbourhood.

So let's say your chosen step is 'Find and make one new friend'. You can always repeat the process when you've succeeded.

Step 2: Think of creative ways to tackle the first step

Here's how your list of creative ideas might go:
- List the people you know already that you'd like to be a friend.
- List the people who you haven't spoken to or hung out with for a while.
- Stop eating alone in the canteen and sit with other people.
- Ask people you know to introduce you to other people.
- Join a club or society. If it involves sports or fitness, you could crack two problems at once!

Step 3: Choose an idea and make a plan to do it

Let's choose idea 1 (List the people you know already that you'd like to be a friend) and make a plan.

- Look up the phone numbers, email and street addresses of old friends.
- Make a list of the people who you met briefly and those who you added on social media or swapped numbers with but have never contacted.
- If you have no way of contacting them but you know their name, add them on social media with a friendly message. Now take a look at those whose numbers you do have, and those who are already your social media friends.
- Choose one person and text or call them up, or send them a message on social media. Invite them to study with you, go for coffee or go for a walk. If they are someone you know from work or college, ask them a question about a difficult piece of work.
- Repeat this process with the next person on your list.

Step 4: Check the plan and put it into action

Check the plan using the Review sheet you saw earlier, and if you have 5 ticks, go for it.

And remember, if this plan doesn't work out, or it gets too much for you in the middle, don't beat yourself up, just go back to your list of creative ideas, and pick another idea to try! *You can do it!*

I NEED TO REVISE FOR EXAMS

Step 1: Choose a single small goal

Almost everyone gets worried about exams - so much to do, so many subjects to revise that it's hard to know where to get started.

This is where viewing this big problem as a series of smaller goals really helps. Don't try and revise everything, just do one subject at a time. So the chunks could be: History / Geography / English / Maths / Science…and so on. Which one to choose first? Let's say History – So that's Step 1.

Step 2: Think of creative ways to tackle the first step

A creative time thinking about ways to revise History could come up with ideas like these:

- Get a copy of the History syllabus and read the topics one by one.
- Make a timetable so that you cover everything in time for the exam.
- Find a friend who's doing the same exam and work together.
- Divide the week into revision periods and don't go out or watch TV at those times.
- Decide on three days a week for revision and turn your phone off at these times.
- Pitch a tent in the garden so you can do all your revision in there, away from the TV.
- Go to the library and get some books out about revision technique.
- Go and stay with a relative who doesn't have a good broadband connection.

Step 3: Choose an idea and make a plan to do it

Let's say you choose idea 3 – find a friend and work together. This is what their plan could include:

- Call your friends in the same class, one by one, and outline the idea.
- Do a deal with the first one who agrees.
- Get together and decide on a day to start work.
- Decide on a place to work.
- Discuss the revision methods you will use - e.g. testing each other?
- Have a plan for when motivation fades.
- Discuss and agree a system of small rewards for good work. Maybe go to the cinema once a week.

Step 4: Check the plan and put it into action

Check the plan for 5 ticks and put it into action. And remember, you will need motivation, especially when you've done the first couple of subjects and are switching to a topic you don't like. Here are some of the things you could stick on the wall to remind you why you why you are doing this:

- Better exam results can mean a better career and more money.
- Poor exam results may mean you'll have to do it all again next year.
- By working harder you increase the chances of a good result.
- You'll feel great when you've done each subject and feel you have done yourself justice.
- Also, you should plan something good to look forward to after the exams.

You can do it!

NOW IT'S YOUR TURN!

As the real life examples show, the Easy 4-Step Plan works really well. All you have to do is take it step by step and be steady and determined.

If one of the ready-made plans you've just seen fits the bill, please use it!

If you need to make one for yourself, get that piece of paper now and start breaking your big problems into bits!

You can get added advice and support by working through the free linked online modules at www.llttf.com. When you've sorted out your current problem, you might want to choose another chapter and work on something else in your life.

Remember to work on your problem bit by bit using the Easy 4-Step and Planner/Review sheets to plan each step one at a time. You can download more worksheets for free from www.llttf.com.

Go for it!

Introduction to Chapter 6

Can you think of someone you know who is really confident? It might be someone on television, or in a band? Or maybe a footballer or sports personality? What is it about them that makes them stand out as confident?

Is it how they stand? What they say or how they say it? Or is their confidence communicated through their clothes, hair or life style? Many of us look up to people like that, admire them and want to be more like them. The key to being you isn't to try and act and be like someone else. Instead, it's about being confident enough to let the real you come out.

This chapter will help you discover the origins of confidence. The things that have been said to you that have encouraged you and given you confidence, or have drained confidence and left you with doubts. The good news is that we're learning new things all the time, and that can be true of confidence too. So, you just need to learn to trust and remind yourself of the many things that make you an OK person. You don't have to be a star to shine and be comfortable in yourself.

You will learn some positive things to remind yourself of whenever you feel small. You'll also get to practice some skills that will build your confidence to express yourself and present yourself well.

Finally, you'll also learn about the advantages and disadvantages of having high standards. High standards can push people to achieve good things. However high standards can also bring consequences. It can be stressful trying to live up to such standards, especially if you're struggling just now and feel under pressure. Instead, you'll learn that good enough is good enough.

You have the power to choose.

Chapter 6

BUILDING
INNER
CONFIDENCE

I JUST CAN'T DO IT

I'm boring

I don't fit in

People don't like me

I'm not good looking

I'm not like everyone else

I MESS EVERYTHING UP

I don't like me

I keep making mistakes

Who says you're not good enough?

You weren't born thinking 'I'm not good enough'. Someone or something made you think and feel that way, perhaps a long time ago.

Maybe it was something your parents said, or didn't say? Perhaps your classmates were cruel about your shape, size or abilities. Maybe you expect so much of yourself that you are never really satisfied with what you do.

Whichever way the idea got into your head, the fact is it's there now, and it's been rattling around for so long that you believe it.

When you have low confidence, you start to behave as if the negative thoughts you learned are true. Hiding away, not trying new things, pushing people away, keeping quiet about what you want, apologising all the time, not bothering to look after yourself. All of which means you don't live or enjoy your life as much as you could.

But you can change. This chapter contains an easy plan for replacing bad ideas (like 'I'm no good at things') with much more sensible ones (like 'I'm alright really').

Turn the page and see what happens

WELL DONE!

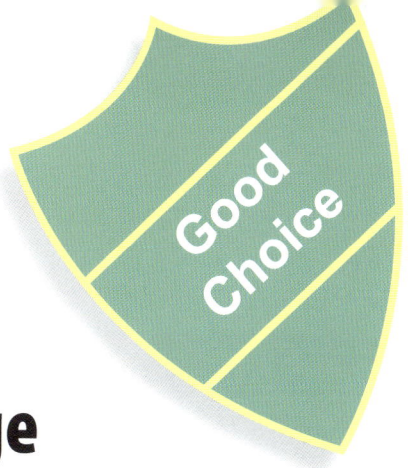

You chose to make a change

Keep doing that and your problems will soon be over.

How come? Well because it's so easy to believe ideas like "I'm useless" or "I'll never change". But these are just unhelpful ideas that got in your head a while ago. If a different idea had got in there instead, like "I'm alright really", you'd feel a lot happier about yourself.

So what we're going to do in the next few pages is show you how to develop positive ideas about yourself, and put them into your head, where they should have been all along.

Then, when you have a choice of things to believe, you can pick a helpful one, like you did a minute ago.

Sounds simple, doesn't it? So, what are you going to do?

Keep reading - because change occurs step by step

YOU'RE GETTING GOOD AT THIS

So let's get some positive ideas going

If we told you the earth is flat, you might not believe us, because you've been abroad and didn't drop off the edge. You have evidence.

It's the same with ideas about yourself. It's hard to believe "I'm alright really" when you don't think you've got any evidence for it. So the first step in your plan is to spot some OK things about yourself and write them down.

Things you did well. Times you were helpful to others. Times you did something even when it was hard. Things you do that people thank you for. Things you know a lot about. Things you can do easily or quickly. Times when you make a good contribution to a group activity. People who like you... and more.

Turn over and list some OK things about yourself

Well done!

You turned to the OK Things list! It may take a while to come up with good stuff, because you've lost the habit of thinking you're OK. You are, though, so get writing!

Things I like about me

Download from

www.llttf.com/resources

* Remember, we're looking for things you did well, times when you were helpful to others, people who like you and so on.

NOW LEARN YOUR LIST BY HEART

And say it to yourself whenever you feel small

You now have a list of reasons to believe you're OK, and every one is real and true, unlike those "I'm no good" ideas that sometimes come into your head.

Learn the list, and add more things to it as you think of them.

I'M OK
I'M OK

Keep repeating it so that it really sticks in your mind. Say it to yourself before going to sleep. Recite it quietly when you have a moment to yourself.

After a while, it will help to replace some of the negative ideas that have been hanging around for so long.

Even better, you can also use your list in emergencies, whenever you get into a situation that makes you feel small.

Just read the list over and over again and it will start to change the other stuff. It's just like you did on the last few pages, choosing a more sensible option instead of the "I'm useless" one.

Over the page is a chart that could help you even more.

Turn over for more help

DON'T THINK THIS

I can't do it

I'm not good looking

I'm boring

People don't like me

I'm not good at things

I mess everything up

THINK
THIS

I can do it because I did
(something from your list)

I look just fine

I'm interesting, I know about
(something from your list)

Some people like me

I have strengths and weaknesses like everyone does

I'm good at ....
(something from your list)

So you know how to change how you think

What's next?

CHANGE WHAT YOU DO

How to build your confidence step by step

Everyone has an inside and an outside, and they're different.

You know those people who seem so confident? They're just like you inside, but they know a trick - walk confidently, talk confidently and you slowly *become* confident.

So what you need to do is be yourself and make some small, steady changes to let the real you shine.

To begin with, take a good look at how you come over to others. Think about:

1. What you wear.
2. How you stand.
3. What you say, and how you say it.

You'll also need to become very observant.

Now you get to make some changes

STEPS TO IMPROVING YOUR CONFIDENCE

How do other people do it?

Watch the way confident people stand. It's straight, isn't it? They often seem a bit taller than they really are.

Now pay attention to the way they hold themselves and move. There's no shuffling about, no slumping in chairs, no hiding in corners. And when they're speaking to you, they look you directly in the eye.

Now listen to the way they speak. They speak out clearly, don't they? And they often speak quite slowly, not having to rush because they somehow know that everyone will keep on listening.

Your task is to slowly work towards this so people see the real you.

Remember, most confident people aren't like that all the way through. They just know how to act confidently on the outside, which is what you'll be doing.

After a while you'll start to notice a real difference in how you present yourself and therefore start to feel better on the inside as well.

Turn over for more helpful hints

DON'T DO THIS

Mumble

Talk too quickly

Slump in your chair, hunch over

Look away or look down

Shut down conversations

DO
THIS

Try to speak a little louder and clearer

Slow down and pause while speaking

Sit up straight, shoulders back

Walk tall, lift your chin up

Make eye contact with others as much as possible, and smile

Ask questions to get conversations going*

*(for example what, where, when, how and who questions can really help get conversations going). For example "*What* did you do at the weekend", "*Where* did you go", "*Who* did you see", "*How* was the meal" etc.

AM I UP TO THIS?

Yes, you are!

It sounds like a lot to do, doesn't it?
To change your thinking and then start
practising ways to become a more
confident you.

But you only have to do these things a
little bit at first. Make that list of things you
like about yourself, and remind yourself
of it when you feel small. Pick a confident
person and notice how they act.

You won't become the life and soul of the
party overnight and you might not even
want to be that loud and bouncy anyway.

You're not here to become a celebrity or a
famous actor.

It's more about finding new ways to act
more confidently, but do it in your own
style.

This way to a very
important thing

GOOD ENOUGH IS GOOD ENOUGH

Don't beat yourself up

In the real world, you don't have to get straight A's to be happy, successful and popular.

In fact the world's happiest people are those who are content with themselves as they are.

So whenever you're being hard on yourself for not doing something perfectly, not coming top of the class or finishing first in the race, say this to yourself:

> There's no such thing as perfect. Just do what you can do.

YOU'RE DOING FINE

Here's how to stay that way

1. Choose sensible ideas not unhelpful ones.
Fill in your list of things you like about you, learn it by heart and use it to change the negative ideas in your head.

Remind yourself of it before going to sleep. Use the list in situations that make you feel small and choose the "I'm OK" idea, not the "I'm useless" one.

2. Walk and talk with confidence.
Remember, most confident people aren't like that all the way through, they just know how to *act* confident on the outside.

So, do the same. Walk confident, talk confident, look confident and you'll slowly become more confident.

3. Remember, there is no such thing as perfect. Just do what you can.
Nobody's perfect, so don't beat yourself up because you can't reach an impossible goal.

So, here's what to do. Pick one small thing, then use the *Planner* sheet on the next two pages to give yourself the best start.

Once you're done, use the *Review* sheet that follows to check your progress.

Go for it!

Planner Sheet

Make a Plan!

1. What am I going to do?

Just one small thing

2. When am I going to do it?

That way you'll know if you don't do it

3. What problems or difficulties could happen, and how can I overcome them?

From the:
**Living life to the full
resources.**

Download from

www.llttf.com/resources

4. Is my planned task -

	Yes	No
• Useful for understanding or changing how I am?		
• Specific, so that I will know when I have done it?		
• Realistic, practical and achievable?		

My notes:

Copyright Five Areas Resources Ltd (2021). Used under licence.
Download more for free from www.llttf.com/resources

LTTF™
living
life to
the full
www.llttf.com

Review Sheet

How did it go? What did you plan to do?

Did you try to do it?

Yes ☐   No ☐

If yes: What went well?

What didn't go so well?

What have you learned from what happened?

How are you going to apply what you have learned?

From the:
Living life to the full
resources.

Download from

www.llttf.com/resources

If no: What stopped you?

External things (other people, work or home issues etc.)

Internal things (forgot, not enough time, put it off, didn't think I could do it, couldn't see the point etc.)

How can you tackle things differently next time?

Copyright Five Areas Resources Ltd (2021). Used under licence.
Download more for free from www.llttf.com/resources

Introduction to Chapter 7

We probably all would like to think we deal with life's challenges in effective and planned ways. Taking the long view and making the healthy choice. But also, if we're honest, that's not always the case. There may be decisions that we each make that make sense as a short term fix, but which come back to cause problems down the line.

There are many choices in life. Some of the most important choices are around when is there too much of a good thing. Think about ice-cream. A single cone is great. Maybe a double cone with the sprinkles on top? Or you could add a chocolate flake? But how many ice-creams can you have at once without feeling sick? Two? Four? What about 24?

There are other life examples like this where something can be healthy, normal and a good thing to do in moderation. So, if someone wants to ask the opinion of a trusted friend about some piece of work they have done, that can be really helpful – and provide useful and constructive feedback. But what if someone starts to feel anxious and doubts themselves and what they do. As a result they start to ask all their friends what they think. They doubt their own choice and keep changing things based on others opinions. Soon their confidence drops even more and they fall into a cycle of seeking reassurance again and again. To start with, their friends are happy to comment, but that good will can wear thin when the same question is asked for the 17th time that day.

There are lots of other life choices like this- where the key is to decide how to make sensible choices about what we do. This chapter will help you discover what makes a choice helpful or unhelpful, and help you identify early signs that difficulties are occurring.

Above all, remember, you have choices to make as to how you choose to respond – helpfully or unhelpfully. Your choice.

Chapter 7

THE THINGS YOU DO THAT HELP ... AND THE THINGS YOU DO THAT DON'T

HIDING AWAY

Eating for Comfort

Binge drinking

Spending too much

Hitting out at people

Checking again and again

BEING CLINGY

COMPLAINING

TAKING RISKS

Gossiping

Seeking reassurance all the time

If it makes me feel better, why should I stop?

"Just leave me alone" or "What I need now is chocolate!" We've all said it, and most of the time it's not a problem at all.

But when you're feeling down, the things that get you through can also become the things that make things worse.

Being alone ends up isolating us. One bar of chocolate becomes a comfort eating habit. One drink becomes a whole bottle. One scratch becomes a cycle of risky self-harm. One question "Are you still my friend?" becomes a constant need for reassurance.

And instead of getting better, you get worse.

But this doesn't need to happen! Turn the page and you'll be taking the first step towards getting in control of the things you do.

YOU'RE ON YOUR WAY!

The first step is the most important

And you just took it. You made the decision to build helpful choices into your life.

Now, we're going to help you work out what you're doing too much of, and then show you a simple 4-step way to stop or cut down.

How do you know when something is making things worse?

Turn over

IT ISN'T WHAT YOU DO, IT'S HOW MUCH YOU DO IT

We're not here to be killjoys. There's nothing wrong with chocolate, spending some time alone, or a bit of retail therapy.

But when you're feeling low, you can start to lean on these things, using them to help get you through a bad time.

Other, not so obvious behaviours can also be 'props'. Like hitting out at people – physically or by shouting. Hurting yourself in different ways. Hiding away from the world.

Trouble is, too much of this kind of stuff makes you worse, not better. You get into a kind of vicious cycle, doing something that seems to help for a bit, but finding that it actually makes life worse in the long run.

Are you doing too much of something?

Think of this like a traffic light.

Drinking

None, or occasional alcohol at home at a family meal (>16 years)	Drinking every day, sometimes getting drunk	Getting really drunk when you're down - drinking most days

Eating for comfort

Eating chocolate etc. occasionally / when you feel upset	Over-eating when you feel upset	Bingeing on food when you're upset

Spending Too Much

Buying some things you just fancy to cheer yourself up	Getting into debt – but under control	Run out of credit and overwhelmed by debt

Taking risks

Seeing occasional risks as exciting	You take more dangerous risks and start to get minor injuries	You do things that would put you in hospital or be fatal if they went wrong

Complaining

You say clearly what you feel and need. You may complain sometimes.	You complain a lot if you don't get your own way	You get very angry and frustrated, and fall out with everyone

Being clingy

| You seek others opinions sometimes | You lean on others a lot of the time | You can't face anything alone |

Hitting out at people

| You're sometimes abrupt with others when frustrated | You begin to throw your weight around and demand your own way | You hit out at people when you feel frustrated and get into fights |

Gossiping

| You tell others good news about your friends | You discuss good news told in confidence | You get a reputation as someone who can't keep things to themselves. People stop telling you things |

Shoplifting

| Your friends say they shoplift and you don't tell them it's wrong | You're with friends when they steal and don't say anything | You take something small and this then escalates |

Hiding away

| You tend to be quiet in conversations | You cross the road to avoid chats with people you know | You lose confidence and find it hard even knowing where to start a conversation |

Want to stop or cut down? **Turn over!**

OK
SO YOU
NEED TO
WORK ON
SOMETHING

Here's how...

First, don't beat yourself up. Most people get into a cycle of doing unhelpful things when they're feeling down or stressed. It's bad for you, and often for other people too.

The fact that you're reading this means you're on the way to fixing it.

All you have to do is choose one problem behaviour to work on, and follow our Easy 4-Step Plan (E4SP for short) to get control.

First choose a problem

The Things You Do That Make Things Worse

Are you:	Tick	My notes:
Are you eating too many sweet things?		
Sitting around all day?		
Spending too much or little?		
Are you not taking your tablets as prescribed?		
Keeping worries to yourself?		
Looking to others for help all the time?		
Lashing out at people?		
Trusting people you don't really know?		
Are you overdoing the phone calls or social media?		
Hiding away?		

Copyright Five Areas Resources Ltd (2021). Used under licence.
Download more for free from www.llttf.com/resources.

From the:
Living life to the full
resources.

Download from

www.llttf.com/resources

Being impulsive about important things?	☐	
Setting yourself up to fail / be rejected?	☐	
Becoming a TV / Internet addict?	☐	
Wanting others to sort out every problem?	☐	
Doing, doing, doing, so you have no time to stop, think and reflect?	☐	
Drinking too much alcohol/coffee/cola to pick yourself up?	☐	
Sleeping in the whole day?	☐	
Putting things off?	☐	
Worrying all the time?	☐	
Other: please write any other things you do that make things worse here:		

This way to something good

225

NOW CHOOSE SOMETHING TO DO THAT HELPS

Choose a helpful response

Just one tiny change to what you do and how you react can make all the difference.

Like what?

Well, how about planning and preparing for a good night's sleep. Or why not try doing something that gives you a lift, such as a hobby, having a relaxing bath, or listening to music? Pick something that you think you might feel motivated to do, and of course something that you think you could keep working at.

There are many helpful things that you could do. Choose one or more that you might do instead of the things you do that make things worse.

Helpful things checklist ahead!

The Things You Do That Help

Are you:	Tick	My notes:
Eating regularly and healthily?	☐	
Giving yourself time to sleep?	☐	
Keeping up with routine things like your household chores?	☐	
Doing things with people you like?	☐	
Doing things you enjoy?	☐	
Sharing problems with trusted friends and family?	☐	
Learning more about how you feel and how to change things?	☐	
Letting upsetting thoughts just be?	☐	

Copyright Five Areas Resources Ltd (2021). Used under licence.
Download more for free from www.llttf.com/resources.

228

From the:
Living life to the full
resources.

Download from
www.llttf.com/resources

Facing your fears in a step by step way? ☐

Doing exercise / going for walks / swimming etc? ☐

Using your sense of humour to cope? ☐

Planning time for you as well as for others? ☐

Regularly taking any medicine prescribed by your doctor? ☐

Relaxing - with music, a film, a book or whatever works for you? ☐

Asking for help from people around you? ☐

Doing the essentials - school/work, looking after yourself etc.? ☐

Q: Am I doing other things that help? Write in what you are doing if this applies to you.

Now, use the Easy 4-Step plan to make changes.

E4SP this way

229

Choose a single small goal

Look back at The Things You Do That Make Things Worse worksheet (6 pages previously). This lists possible unhelpful behaviours. If you have identified quite a few, it's important to start by choosing just one to focus on.

Pick something that is making you feel worse emotionally, physically, or is unhelpfully affecting your relationships.

So, if you've lost your confidence and are hiding away from the world, what could you do? You could break the week into bits and decide to do something with someone else on Mondays, for example.

Don't try and become a party animal yet - just work on a little bit of the problem - like getting out of the house.

Or if you're spending too much, start by just cutting out online shopping.

Most problems can be chopped up like this, and you're much more likely to succeed when you do things bit by bit.

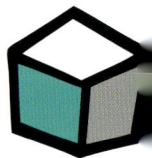

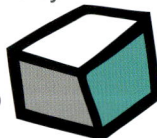

Think of creative ways to tackle the first step

Download from

www.llttf.com/resources

Grab a piece of paper and write down all the things you could do to work on the first bit of the problem.

To meet up with somebody on Mondays, for example, you could ask a friend round, meet one or more people somewhere quiet and comfortable, or try something small like an email, phone call or text. Do anything that reconnects you to others and moves things on.

The trick is to be creative and let your mind go. Write everything down - the ridiculous things as well as the sensible ones.

Do this and there's bound to be a good idea in there somewhere.

TURN OVER FOR STEPS 3 and 4

Phone or text a friend

Meet just one person

Meet a few

Choose an idea and make a plan to do it

Look at your list of ideas and pick one that looks do-able. Remember, to make a big change in your life you are best chunking this into a series of smaller pieces. Make sure that the steps are small, straightforward and seem like things you could really do.

Choose something that is:
• Useful for understanding or changing how you are.
• Specific, so that you will know when you have done it.
• Realistic, practical and achievable.

Make each step as small as you like.

Now plan out what you'll do and when.
• *What* are you going to do?
• *When* are you going to do it?

Make sure your plan doesn't push you too far or too fast. Make it slow and easy to do so you move forward step by step.

Going to meet on Monday? You need to get it arranged a day or so before. On the Saturday, text your friend and ask them round on Monday evening. Ask them to let you know if they can make it, or whether another time is better.

What if something gets in the way?

As soon as you've written your plan, think about what could stop it happening. Is there anything that might trip you up?
• What could happen, and how can you overcome any problems?

When you know what could block your progress, make a mini-plan for getting round the block. This way, you'll be ready for whatever happens!

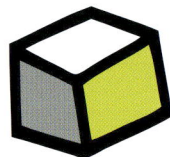

Check the plan and put it into action

This is it! You've made your plan, now you need to check that it's do-able. Use this checklist:

Is it just one thing?
You're not planning to change everything all at once.

Are you aiming at just one thing?
Don't try and do more than one item on your list. You can always pick another when you've sorted out the first one.

Is it slow?
There's no need to rush at things. Your plan can take as long as you like, so long as you stick to it, step by step.

Is it easy?
Make your steps small and easy and you'll be more likely to do them.

Are you ready to unblock it?
Have you thought about what could go wrong and how to deal with it?

FIVE TICKS?

THEN GO FOR IT!

NOW KEEP IT GOING!

Just take it step by step

Even a problem that seems huge can be tackled with the E4SP. The secret is breaking everything down into small, manageable steps.

When you're making your plan, be sure that the steps are small and do-able. Plan to cut down unhelpful behaviours and replace them with helpful ones.

When you're doing your plan, take it step by step and if things get scary in the middle, give yourself a rest or a breather. If it seems too much - take a step back and do something a bit easier for a time.

Then get back on track, until you've put your plan into action.

Be steady and determined, use the E4SP and you will be able to stop doing the things that backfire, and build more helpful responses.

Use the Planner sheet on the next two pages to help you plan these changes. Then complete the Review sheet on the two pages that follow to complete the pattern of Plan- Do-Review.

Go for it!

Planner Sheet

Make a Plan!

1. What am I going to do?

Just one small thing

2. When am I going to do it?

That way you'll know if you don't do it

3. What problems or difficulties could happen, and how can I overcome them?

From the:
Living life to the full resources.

Download from

www.llttf.com/resources

4. Is my planned task –

	Yes	No
• Useful for understanding or changing how I am?	☐	☐
• Specific, so that I will know when I have done it?	☐	☐
• Realistic, practical and achievable?	☐	☐

My notes:

Copyright Five Areas Resources Ltd (2021). Used under licence.
Download more for free from www.llttf.com/resources.

Review Sheet

living life to the full
www.llttf.com

How did it go? What did you plan to do?

Did you try to do it?

Yes ☐   No ☐

If yes: What went well?

What didn't go so well?

What have you learned from what happened?

How are you going to apply what you have learned?

238

From the:
Living life to the full
resources.

Download from

www.llttf.com/resources

If no: What stopped you?

External things (other people, work or home issues etc.)

Internal things (forgot, not enough time, put it off, didn't think I could do it, couldn't see the point etc.)

How can you tackle things differently next time?

Copyright Five Areas Resources Ltd (2021). Used under licence.
Download more for free from www.llttf.com/resources

Introduction to Chapter 8

Do you always stay calm? Relaxed when someone spills their drink over your mobile phone? Happy when someone says something bad about you to others? Unless you're a Saint (and we think even Saints lose their tempers sometimes!) there will probably be things every day or every week that make us feel annoyed.

Anger can sometimes be appropriate. If something unjust happens it's entirely healthy and normal to get annoyed – things like poverty, injustice, inequality ... the list goes on of things we should all be angry about. However whether that anger is productive and helpful is also about the choices we make in how we respond.

How we choose to respond when we feel annoyed really matters. Do we lose control and throw a tantrum? Do we shout, or swear or lash out? When we lose control like that we might feel powerful for a time- but in the longer term we can end up becoming isolated. People move away and give us a wide berth, they may be wary of us, and we can feel bad because we lost it rather than responding maturely.

So, how can we slow things down when we start to get angry so we respond in better ways? Mature ways that solve problems rather than adding to them? Again, it involves choices – choices to respond differently. This chapter tells you how to do this and gain control so your anger works for you rather than against you.

Chapter 8

1, 2, 3
BREATHE

Don't laugh at me

Turn that music down!

She just pushes my buttons

GOT A PROBLEM WITH THAT?

You never listen

DON'T ANSWER ME BACK

YOU MAKE ME DO THIS!

Are you looking at me?

He was asking for it

DON'T TALK TO ME LIKE THAT!

He really winds me up

Excuses, excuses

What 'reason' do you use when you fly off the handle?

Did someone else say something, do something or forget to do something? Maybe you got into an argument and the other person wouldn't listen. Did a family member or a neighbour make too much noise? Was it a child, brother, sister or friend that pushed your buttons?

Whatever your excuse, and however much you feel like lashing out at the time, the truth is, getting angry gets you nowhere.

Except into trouble, into hospital, and out of relationships. Lose your temper all the time and you'll probably lose everything, eventually.

And anyway, temper tantrums get you nowhere.

They're what you do when you lose it. When all you can think of is throwing your toys out of the pram. When you don't know the difference between being strong and being aggressive.

Know what we think?

IT'S WEAK TO STAY AND SHOUT

Doesn't sound right, does it?

A lot of people say that standing your ground is strong, that you should look up to people who don't take any nonsense.

But think about it. What happens when you lose your temper? Things get out of control and you get into trouble. People steer clear of you. You end up on your own.

What's so strong about that?

Wouldn't it be better NOT to shout and lash out? Wouldn't it be better to be admired for being calm and in control?

This chapter can help you do that, but you'll have to be strong. A lot stronger than your angry self.

Strong stuff next

IT'S STRONG TO KEEP YOUR COOL

Choose to react differently

Strong, calm, controlled people choose to avoid aggravation in the first place, or they choose to react differently when they feel their hackles start to rise.

It takes real strength to do this. It's much easier to lose it, shout or swear, stamp your feet or throw a punch.

But this chapter will help you take the tougher option. When you use the 3-step plan that comes later, you'll really get to know your own temper and how to keep it under control.

You'll become calmer, quieter, more powerful. And the people who count will know that you're a much stronger person than you used to be.

247

YOU GOT A PROBLEM WITH THAT?

It's not strong to lose control

If you still think losing control of yourself isn't a bad idea, think about this:

Imagine you're driving a fast car and you come to a tight bend with a slippery surface. You're going to need all your skill to stay on the road, so you take a deep breath, remember everything you've learned about driving, grip the wheel and control the car until the danger is past.

What would happen if you lost control, instead? If you let a red mist come down and you got angry at the bend because it was too tight? You'd skid, wouldn't you? You, the car and your passengers would end up in the ditch, in the hospital or in the graveyard.

In your life, you're always in that car. Your aim is to finish your journey in one piece. That slippery bend is just something that 'pushes your buttons'.

Use your skill to stay in control. Lose your temper and you don't.

Now ask what's in it for you

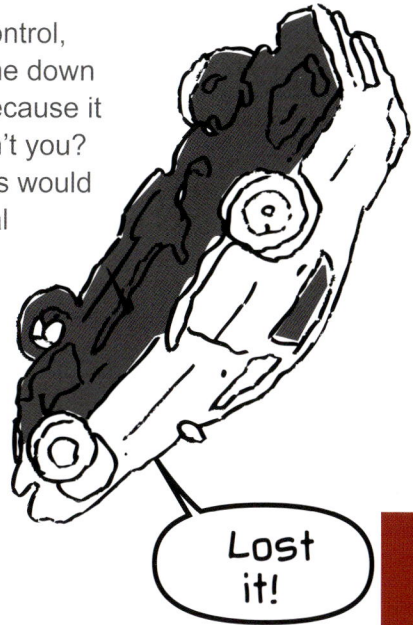

Lost it!

WHAT'S IN IT FOR ME?

Big respect

The self-respect you earn when you stay in control and use your skill and strength to handle a tough situation.

The respect of your friends and family who look at you in a new way and start to realise that you're stronger than they thought.

The respect of strangers who, when you speak calmly or walk away from angry situations, know that you helped to make things better, not worse.

There's not much that's more important than making good decisions. If you agree, and think you're strong enough to try our 3-step plan, turn the page and…

Let's get started!

IT'S EASY TO BE STRONG

As easy as...

1 ### Know your buttons
Think about what makes you angry. The people or places that always seem to get you going. When you know your buttons, you can keep them from being pressed.

2 ### Know your early warning signs
You feel different just before you snap. With some people it's heavy breathing. Others feel the blood pounding in their ears. Learn to spot these signs so you can move to step 3 before they turn into trouble.

3 ### Know where the escape hatches are
You just decide to react differently this time. Some people pause and count to 10, or decide to walk away. Others have calming words that they say, that de-fuse a situation. When you have a few of these up your sleeve, you'll be able to stay in control whatever happens.

Breathe!

As soon as you've responded differently, give yourself respect. You're strong. You're in control. You've steered the car round that slippery corner without losing it.

You've been strong enough to keep your temper.

So let's do it

KNOW
YOUR
BUTTONS

What always gets you going?

Something someone says at home? What about your friends? Other people? What about when people are noisy around you or tell you what to do?

Is it your brother/sister, a teacher, the government, the police, the environment, or people who are selfish?

What about when you drink? Is it worse then? And when you're having a night out, does just being around certain people make you feel like arguing or fighting?

These are all buttons. You need to think about them so that you know exactly which ones apply to you. Then you need to write them down on the next 2 pages.

Why? Because when you know your buttons, you can keep them from being pressed. Go to different places. Spend time with different people. Ignore other people's comments. Get control of the car, steer round the corner and forget about what other drivers are doing.

This way to the buttons

Download from
www.llttf.com/resources

My Buttons

Write down the things that make you lose your temper or get irritable

What gets me going?

What gets me going?

Step 2 next

KNOW YOUR EARLY WARNING SIGNS

Feeling tense?

Think about the last time you lost your temper. How did you feel just beforehand? Can you remember what happened, physically or mentally?

You may have started breathing heavily, clenched your fists, stood up suddenly, folded your arms, drummed on the table with your fingers. Some people really do see a red mist in front of their eyes.

Or maybe your early warnings are in your mind. You start to feel critical of someone else. You don't think much of their appearance, their voice, their clothes, their opinions. Maybe you feel ignored or think people are looking down on you?

All these signs are really useful, because they warn you that you're getting near to losing it. They're like a road sign that says 'Slippery corner ahead'.

Think about the signs that apply to you and write down as many as you can on the next two pages.

List this way

1 2 3 Breathe!

Download from
www.llttf.com/resources

My Early Warning Signs

Write down all the things you think and feel,
just before you lose it

Feeling hot or breathing hard (for example)

What to do when you start to feel this way

USE THE ESCAPE HATCH

This is when you react differently

Here's when you count to 10, or change the subject, or walk away, or sit down, relax your shoulders and breathe deeply.

Some people 'switch on' some music in their head when they get one of their early warning signs.

Others have a few words that they whisper to take the heat out of the situation ('slippery corner, watch the road ahead' are good ones).

You need to have a choice of escape hatches and be ready to use one whenever you get an early warning sign.

You can invent your own, of course, that fit with the buttons you wrote down earlier. Or you can turn the page and see some of the escape hatches that other people use. They won't mind you borrowing them.

More ideas this way

MORE ESCAPE HATCHES

Walk away

Here's a great solution. If you can, make an excuse and leave before things escalate. You don't need to agree or back down, but choose to leave - maybe saying "Can we talk about this later".

Say "You might be right about that"

This works best when you really disagree with someone. Instead of arguing and getting angry, just say "You might be right about that". You don't have to mean it, it's an escape hatch. Often, the other person will be so surprised that all the tension will drain away. An alternative is to say "I understand what you mean/respect your opinion ... and I'll have a think about it later".

Sit down

When we're about to explode, we need to be standing, so we can fight, or run, or seem bigger than we are.

It's a lot harder to get into trouble when you're sitting down though, so when you get an early warning, stay in your seat, or go find one.

Hum

We're serious. What's your favourite song? Get into the habit of quietly or even silently humming it to yourself when you get an early warning. Use it to change your focus. It works even better with slow, calming tunes.

And finally

BREATHE

Relax your shoulders and breathe slowly

Often, your shoulders go up around your ears when tension builds. If you notice this in time and make a point of relaxing and letting them drop, you'll calm yourself and others too. Breathe slowly and think about those slippery corners while you do it.

When you breathe, close your mouth – it's hard to over-breathe through your nose.

And as you breathe, reconnect with your body and surroundings. Use it to centre yourself – to step back and notice your reactions.

Stop, think and reflect.

Use the breaths to focus and change how you react.

Feels great doesn't it?

1 2 3 Breathe!

SO NEXT TIME

Follow the plan

1 Know your buttons

Get to know the buttons on your list. When you know them, you can keep them from being pressed.

2 Know your early warning signs

Learn your danger signs and look out for them so that you can move to step 3 before they turn into trouble.

3 Know where the escape hatches are

React differently. Count to 10, walk away, say the phrase, hum the tune. Whatever your chosen escapes are, use one as soon as you get an early warning sign.

Breathe!

Now give yourself respect.

You're powerful. You're in control. You've steered the car round that slippery corner without losing it.

You're strong enough to keep your temper! Now, time to make a plan. Pick one small thing to practice or change. Then use the Planner sheet on the next two pages to give yourself the best start.

Once you're done, use the Review sheet that follows to check your progress.

Go, make a plan

Go for it!

Planner Sheet

Make a Plan!

1. What am I going to do?

Just one small thing

2. When am I going to do it?

That way you'll know if you don't do it

3. What problems or difficulties could happen, and how can I overcome them?

From the:
Living life to the full resources.

Download from
www.llttf.com/resources

4. Is my planned task -

	Yes	No
• Useful for understanding or changing how I am?	☐	☐
• Specific, so that I will know when I have done it?	☐	☐
• Realistic, practical and achievable?	☐	☐

My notes:

Copyright Five Areas Resources Ltd (2021). Used under licence.
Download more for free from www.llttf.com/resources

living
life to
the full
LLTTF™
www.llttf.com

Review Sheet

How did it go? What did you plan to do?

Did you try to do it?   Yes ☐   No ☐

If yes: What went well?

What didn't go so well?

What have you learned from what happened?

How are you going to apply what you have learned?

From the:
Living life to the full resources.

Download from

www.llttf.com/resources

If no: What stopped you?

External things (other people, work or home issues etc.)

Internal things (forgot, not enough time, put it off, didn't think I could do it, couldn't see the point etc.)

How can you tackle things differently next time?

Copyright Five Areas Resources Ltd (2021). Used under licence.
Download more for free from www.llttf.com/resources

Introduction to Chapter 9

We all want to feel happier don't we? To enjoy things, to feel and live in healthy ways, and to appreciate the good things around us. But sometimes it can seem so hard. This chapter makes a remarkable claim. That there are some things that we can all choose to do which can help start to make us feel happier straight away. Each of the things are small achievable actions that can have powerful impacts on how we feel.

But setting up new habits can feel hard. Think back to the start of the year and all the New Year Resolutions that each of us can make- and often fail to keep. What causes a failed resolution? Being unrealistic? Maybe trying to do it all by yourself? Maybe beating yourself up mentally if you have a setback? There's so many things that can make change hard. That's why this chapter- and each of the other chapters ends with the idea of making a plan. Having a Plan gives you direction. It helps you plan what you'll do and when you'll do it. That pattern of *Plan, Do* and *Review* (using the Planner and Review sheets) is a pattern you can use to take forward the lessons of this chapter, this book and the linked course at www.llttf.com.

So, as you come to this final topic, remember you have choices and control going forward in your life. Use the Planner and Review sheets to help you make effective plans, so you move forward learning all the time. That way, you really will move towards living life to the full.

Chapter 9

10 THINGS YOU CAN DO TO FEEL HAPPIER STRAIGHT AWAY

(FOR WHEN YOU WANT SOME PRACTICAL THINGS TO MAKE A DIFFERENCE NOW)

Seriously!

No Pills
No Booze
No Drugs
No Diets
No Supplements
No Preaching
No Pain

You can start feeling better about 10 minutes from now

Like loads of people, you're not feeling great at the moment.

Your system's a bit sluggish. You're miserable some of the time. You think your life could be better all round, but nothing seems to cheer you up these days.

So, here's the good news: you can start to feel better in a few minutes from now. All you have to do is finish reading this chapter and then make some small, easy changes to what you do each day.

More good stuff

DON'T PANIC!

No broccoli is involved

You *will* have to get off the couch and walk about a bit. You'll also have to eat more healthily, but you won't have to wear Lycra shorts and we promise you don't have to turn your life upside down.

The thing is this: there are things you can do and things you can eat that can *make you feel happier straight away.*

Amazingly, some foods can help you get going to face the day. Some activities give you a major boost.

When you combine the two – eating *and* doing certain things – those fed up feelings can improve (along with spots and even excess weight sometimes).

And it's easy. You just make ten small changes to your daily routine.

Are you ready?

10
SMALL,
EASY
CHANGES

1. **Get Outside More**

2. **Eat Good Things**

3. **Put On Your WOW Glasses**

4. **Call a Friend**

5. **Get Creative**

6. **Slow It Down**

7. **Make a Note of This**

8. **Take One Away**

9. **Do Something for Someone Else**

10. **The Happy List**

This way to small, easy change No.1

Small Easy change !

GET OUTSIDE MORE

Enjoy the fresh air and exercise

Exercise is good for you. So good that when you do it, your body says 'thanks' by boosting happy chemicals in your brain.

Go for a walk, or enjoy a run. Try high impact training on You Tube, or a class at the local gym. If you enjoy dancing, then dance. Put on the music and show off your moves! Take a dog for a walk. If you don't have one, then try borrowing one from a neighbour - ideally an elderly neighbour who has difficulty walking.

Climbing stairs is one of the best ways there is to get fitter and get that happy stuff into your head. In fact climbing stairs each day for a year is the same as climbing a large mountain. Great view isn't it!

While you're climbing the stairs at the shopping centre, here's what to buy…

EAT GOOD THINGS

Are you fed up with hearing about 5 a day?

Even if you like fruit and vegetables, it's hard to have five portions a day.

Trouble is, you really do need that much fibre. Without it, your system clogs up and you get all sad and sluggish.

So here's a cheat – drink smoothies. Other things can help too like porridge and muesli. They give you lasting energy and keep you regular.

You can also snack on fruit like bananas and strawberries, enjoying the taste, smell and textures.

Ready? Walk briskly to the shop, buy the fruit, veg and muesli you like. Walk briskly home, mix, mash and enjoy your first of five glasses, feel smug.

Got diabetes or watching your weight? Then choose low sugar fruits like berries, cherries, apples, grapefruit, pears, apricots, strawberries and plums.

Small, easy change
No. 3 next

285

PUT ON YOUR 'WOW' GLASSES

The world is amazing when you really look at it

When was the last time you went outside and really noticed what's there? The wind, the warmth, the cold, the rain, the trees, the flowers, the shops and the sky?

When you stop and think, the world is full of stuff that makes you go 'Wow!'

People who recover from really bad times often say they appreciate things they used to take for granted. So, put on your special glasses and see the world for the amazing place it is.

Even better do it with a friend. Go for walks together, talk about good times, and you'll soon get those happy feelings going through your brain.

TEST

IT

OUT

Use the next page to rate your mood before and after your WOW walk.

Use it to discover the effect of your WOW walk (or indeed any altered activity) on you.

Rate Your Mood

Download from
www.llttf.com/resources

Rate how you feel:

Before your walk

Having fun/ Feeling happy

Very bad	Bad	OK	Good	Very good
☐	☐	☐	☐	☐

Feeling tense or stressed

Very bad	Bad	OK	Good	Very good
☐	☐	☐	☐	☐

Getting stuff done/Sense of achievement

Very bad	Bad	OK	Good	Very good
☐	☐	☐	☐	☐

Enjoying being with others

Very bad	Bad	OK	Good	Very good
☐	☐	☐	☐	☐

After your walk

Having fun/ Feeling happy

Very bad	Bad	OK	Good	Very good
☐	☐	☐	☐	☐

Feeling tense or stressed

Very bad	Bad	OK	Good	Very good
☐	☐	☐	☐	☐

Getting stuff done/Sense of achievement

Very bad	Bad	OK	Good	Very good
☐	☐	☐	☐	☐

Enjoying being with others

Very bad	Bad	OK	Good	Very good
☐	☐	☐	☐	☐

Copyright Five Areas Resources Ltd (2021). Used under licence. Download more for free from www.llttf.com/resources

CALL A FRIEND

It's good to talk

Connecting with others that you care about can make you feel good.

It's easy if you feel tired, or stressed, or fed up to hide away. But that just worsens the problem. You feel isolated and have less things to talk about when you do meet up with others.

So, reach out. Pick up the phone, make a call, send a text or an email. Or post an update on social media that's fun and will get others chatting with you.

Small Easy change s

GET CREATIVE

Act like a kid again

It's great to discover the excitement of creating something new that you've thought of and done by yourself.

What are you good at - what do you enjoy?

Drawing, painting, gardening, taking photographs, writing a blog post, keeping a journal, playing or writing music, writing a poem or a rap, creating a mural in your bedroom. Or paint the fence or decking, do some weeding, or plant vegetables, bulbs or flowers.

There's no better feeling than to see the end result.

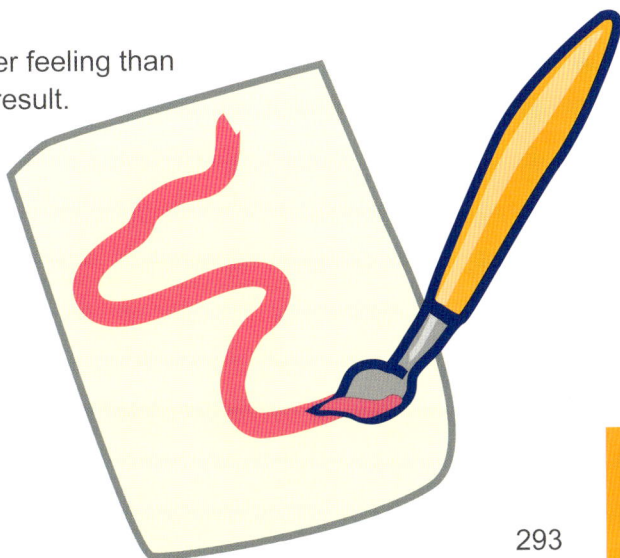

SLOW IT DOWN

Free mindfulness resources

Download from

www.lttf.com/resources

Slow down and Be*...

Try to focus on just one task at a time. So, don't watch television and go on social media at the same time. Put your phone away in your bag or pocket when you are speaking to someone.

- Breathe: drop your shoulders and focus on the breath.

- Choose to sometimes read a book rather than using a phone or computer.

- Take a long, hot bath.

- Take the opportunity to talk and reconnect with people around you. You might find they are feeling the same way and have even more hints and tips you can use too.

Oh, and while doing it ...

You could try the next idea

* if you love the idea of mindfulness, we have a separate book and course available. It's called Slow down and Be.

Small Easy Change 7

MAKE A NOTE OF THIS

Don't suffer in silence

Music cheers you up. Obvious? So why are you sitting there in silence? Silence is just a space for you to think about your worries.

Put some of your favourite music on. Do it now. Play music while you're exercising and getting out of breath and it'll send even more happy feelings to your brain.

Play music while you're walking briskly to the shops. Play music while you're sitting around. Create a "happy" playlist for when you need a boost.

But don't play sad stuff, or songs that remind you of unhappy times. Keep it upbeat and you'll get an instant lift.

TAKE ONE AWAY

This one saves money too

Eating too much fast food or takeaway food is a great way to get really down.

Did you see that experiment where a man ate nothing but fast food? He felt depressed and really unhealthy within a couple of weeks.

So here's what you do: cut out one portion of fast food a week. Just one. Replace it with something you make yourself (easy things like pasta or beans on toast are fine).

It won't change your life all at once, but put together with the extra outdoor activity and healthier eating you're doing and within a few weeks you'll start to feel lighter, fitter and happier. And a bit better off.

DO SOMETHING FOR SOMEONE ELSE

It's not what you do, it's who you do it for

Do a small kindness for someone else and you'll feel even better than they do. What's more, you'll feel good straight away.

It doesn't have to be a big thing like sometimes helping at a food bank or drop-in centre (although those would be great, of course).

You can just as easily get a lift in your mood by helping someone with their work, letting someone know you appreciate their friendship, cooking a meal or spending time with a person who needs the company.

Go on, sit down now and plan one or two helpful things you're going to do for other people this week. They'll feel good, but you'll feel even better!

Final idea coming up next

THE HAPPY LIST

My Good Times

Remember the good things

When you're down it's easy to forget the good times- times you've succeeded in something, happy times with friends, things that make you smile and times you did something to help someone else.

So, plan to remember them. Each evening, sit down and write down three things that you:

- Have enjoyed.

- Felt was a job well done.

- Or helped you feel close to someone else.

After a few days, you'll have a list of great things that you can look back on, and will help you feel a lot better.

What you think about affects how you feel. Focus on the good things and you'll be happier for it!

Try it out

303

MY
GOOD TIMES

Write down all the things you've enjoyed, felt was a job well done, or has helped you feel close to someone else.

How much did it fit with your values/ideals of how you want to live your life? Is there anything to be thankful for?

WHAT ARE YOU WAITING FOR?

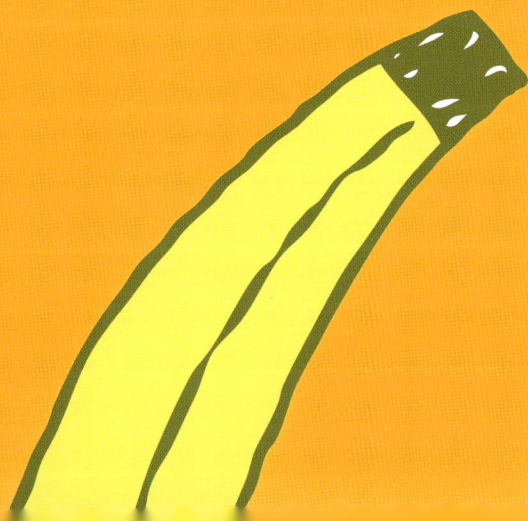

Go and get that banana

At the beginning of this chapter, we promised you could start feeling better in ten minutes. It's time, so here's what to do:

Pick one small thing then use the Planner sheet on the next two pages to give yourself the best start.

For example, if it's daylight, go out, walk briskly to the corner shop and buy a couple of bananas. Walk quickly home and make a smoothie.

If it's night and the shops are closed, walk up and down your stairs or jog on the spot for ten minutes, or long enough to get your heart pumping.

Whichever you do, you'll know you're making changes that make a difference.

Once you're done, use the Review sheet that follows to check your progress.

Go for it!

LTTF™
living
life to
the full
www.llttf.com

Planner Sheet

Make a Plan!

1. What am I going to do?

Just one small thing

2. When am I going to do it?

That way you'll know if you don't do it

3. What problems or difficulties could happen, and how can I overcome them?

From the:
Living life to the full
resources.

Download from

www.llttf.com/resources

4. Is my planned task -

	Yes	No
• Useful for understanding or changing how I am?		
• Specific, so that I will know when I have done it?		
• Realistic, practical and achievable?		

My notes:

Copyright Five Areas Resources Ltd (2021). Used under licence.
Download more for free from www.llttf.com/resources

living
life to
the full
www.llttf.com

Review Sheet

How did it go? What did you plan to do?

Did you try to do it?   Yes [ ]   No [ ]

If yes: What went well?

What didn't go so well?

What have you learned from what happened?

How are you going to apply what you have learned?

From the:
Living life to the full
resources.

Download from

www.llttf.com/resources

If no: What stopped you?

External things (other people, work or home issues etc.)

Internal things (forgot, not enough time, put it off, didn't think I could do it, couldn't see the point etc.)

How can you tackle things differently next time?

Copyright Five Areas Resources Ltd (2021). Used under licence.
Download more for free from www.llttf.com/resources

WHERE TO GET EVEN MORE HELP

(but no broccoli)

For more tips on feeling better, go to www.llttf.com. It's free and the number one site for low mood and anxiety recommended by NHS Trusts and teams in England.* It is also recommended by the National Wellbeing Hub for Scotland www.promis.scot/resource/coping-and-self-care/

It's packed with ways to lift your mood and start having a happier and healthier life.

And don't worry, last time we looked, very few vegetables were mentioned.

*Bennion et al, 2017. BMJ Open http://bmjopen.bmj.com/content/7/1/e014844

LOOK OUT FOR MORE RESOURCES LIKE THIS

The Worry Box for Young People

Discover the causes of worry, panic and more. Written especially for older teenagers (Year 3 secondary school and above), this book helps readers understand then overcome anxiety. Using the three F system- Fix It, Face It, Forget It, key life skills needed to overcome problems, tackle phobias and avoidance, and challenge catastrophic fears are taught in a clear empowering way.

This resource also contains a chapter to help beat panic attacks.

Free help for dental anxiety in teenagers: www.llttf.com/dental

A guide for young people who aren't keen to visit the dentist. With easy resources designed by young people for young people, you can learn how to feel happier and attend dental appointments with a plan.

Jargon free and accessible. Clear, practical and helpful advice written by the award-winning team behind some of the world's most used CBT resources.

Linked book Highly Commended BMA Patient Information Awards.

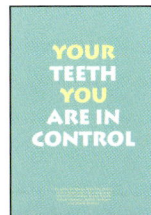

My Big Life Classes www.llttfyp.com

For younger teenagers in transition (final year primary and first two years of secondary school). Can be used as a universal or targeted support course. Attractive content and worksheets support young people who feel they are struggling to live the life they want to.

313

living
life to
the full
Resources

Feel happier? Gain confidence?

Overcome problems?

Become more assertive?

Feel calmer in the face of frustration?

Respond better to upset and stress?

Sleep more peacefully?

Living life to the Full is one of the world's most recommended self-help systems. Over 1,750,000 books sold, an award-winning website and books available in over 15 language. Courses and worksheets are available for use by people across the life span.

Course content is available in three forms to suit how people want to learn:

For details visit www.llttf.com/shop